TECHNOLOGY: BLUEPRINTS OF THE FUTURE

TECHNOLOGY:
BLUEPRINTS OF THE FUTURE

Large Telescopes

Inside and Out

by
Ray Villard

Illustrations
Alessandro Bartolozzi, Leonello Calvetti, Lorenzo Cecchi

The Rosen Publishing Group's
PowerPlus Books ™
New York

This book is dedicated to my loving family: my wife Paulette, and children Renee, Eric, and Chris,
who have all shared in my awe and wonder of the universe. It is dedicated to my mother and father who fostered
my early interest in astronomy with trips to the Hayden Planetarium, looking for Sputnik, *and building a*
toy model of the famous Hale telescope. And finally I want to dedicate this book to those professionals
whose unwavering encouragement, trust, and support provided me with the opportunities to make astronomy
communication a career: Harold Buchbinder, Jack Carr, Terry Dickinson, Dan Zirpoli,
Mark Littmann, Eric Chaisson, Riccardo Giacconi.

Copyright © 2002
by Andrea Dué s.r.l., Florence, Italy, and
Rosen Book Works, Inc., New York, USA

Published in 2002 in North America
by The Rosen Publishing Group, Inc., New York

First Edition

Book Design:
Andrea Dué s.r.l. Florence, Italy

Illustrations:
Alessandro Bartolozzi, Leonello Calvetti, Lorenzo Cecchi,
Luigi Ieracitano, Roberto Simoni, Studio Stalio

Editor and Photo Researcher:
Joanne Randolph

Associate Editor:
Jason Moring

Library of Congress Cataloging-in-Publication Data

Villard, Ray.
Large telescopes : inside and out / by Ray Villard. — 1st ed.
p. cm. — (Technology: blueprints of the future)
Includes bibliographical references and index.
ISBN 0-8239-6110-9 (library binding)
1. Telescopes—Juvenile literature. [1. Telescopes.] I. Title. II. Series.
QB90 .V55 2002
522'.29—dc21
2001001114
Manufactured in Italy by Eurolitho S.p.A., Milan

Contents

A Journey Back in Time

Telescopes are time machines, literally. They can take you on a journey to when Earth was young, or even to before it existed. You can travel to view the universe as it was when our Milky Way was just forming, or even back to within a few minutes of the big bang, when the first elements were formed.

Telescopes perform these feats not through the artificial special effects of science fiction movies, but by taking advantage of a fundamental aspect of the universe: the finite, or measurable, speed of light. When you flick on a light switch, you don't notice a delay while the light from the bulb makes its way through space to your eyes. It all happens much too fast for your senses to register—in about ten billionths of a second. That's fast, but it is not instantaneous. In fact we have measured the speed of light very precisely: it's 186,000 miles per second (300,000 km/s)—that's about eight times around Earth in one second! Despite its speed, it still takes eight minutes for light to travel from the Sun to Earth. If the Sun stopped shining, we would not know about it for eight minutes!

The distances in astronomy are so vast that the effect of the finite speed of light, completely unimportant in your everyday life, soon starts to become important. It takes more than four hours for light to get to us from the planet Neptune, and more than four years for it to reach us from the nearest star, Proxima Centauri. If you look through a telescope at Proxima Centauri today, you are seeing it not as it is now, but as it was when you were four years younger. Similarly, if you look at the sword of the constellation Orion, you are seeing stars that flared to life not today, but seventeen hundred years ago when the Roman emperor Constantine ruled much of the world.

Turn a telescope toward the Milky Way and you are seeing light that left our galaxy's heart thirty thousand years ago, when Neanderthals huddled in the freezing caves of Ice Age Europe. Look at the great cluster of galaxies in Coma, and you are seeing light that left those galaxies when the dinosaurs walked on Earth.

Top Right: It takes 70 million years for light from the supergiant elliptical galaxies NGC 4889 and NGC 4874 and the 300 smaller elliptical galaxies at the center of the Coma cluster, to reach Earth.

Bottom Right: When light from the Milky Way reaches Earth, it is already 40,000 years old. We are seeing it as it looked in the distant past. Dinosaurs still walked on Earth when the light first left the Milky Way.
Courtesy of LBT Corporation

Below: The chart below explains how long it takes light and information to reach Earth from various parts of space. Telescopes allow us to see light that left these places long ago. For example, it takes 8 minutes for light from the Sun to reach Earth. So, at any given moment, we are seeing the Sun as it looked 8 minutes ago.

THE SUN

8 minutes

EARTH

MOON

more than 4 hours

NEPTUNE

1,700 years

4 years

40,000 years

70 million years

The telescope is coming up on its four hundredth birthday. In that time, technology has taken us from scientist Galileo's two lenses that would fit in the palm of your hand to the huge twin Keck telescopes with three hundred thousand times the light-gathering power. In the last two decades, we have made all telescopes fifty times more sensitive by replacing photographic film (which captures only about 1% of the light that hits it) with electronic cameras that record 90% of the light. The result is that we can now see objects a hundred million times fainter than Galileo could see when he first turned his crude instrument to the sky over northern Italy and launched the modern era of astronomy. We routinely detect single exploding stars halfway across the universe—explosions that occurred before Earth was born. We chart quasars 97% of the way back to the beginning of time, probing what the universe looked like as the first galaxies began to form.

Of course we aren't nearly done. Plans are already underway to build a massive telescope, nearly the size of Keck, that can map the whole sky in a week. Several groups of astronomers are exploring designs that will allow us to build ground-based telescopes big enough to play a regulation football game on the mirror (Although those cleats might really mess up the surface!). The Next Generation Space Telescope (NGST) is just that—a Hubble for the next generation: yours.

Now settle back at the focus of your time machine, and get ready for an exciting ride.

Dr. David Helfand, Professor
Columbia Astrophysics Laboratory
Columbia University

MILKY WAY

ORION

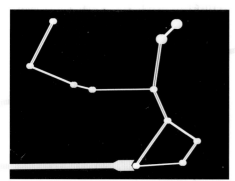

PROXIMA CENTAURI

The Wondrous Telescope

Today we use powerful machines to explore the frontiers of nature. Particle accelerators break atoms into their smallest pieces, rockets hurl roving spacecraft to other planets, and robots prowl the cold, pitch-black depths of the ocean floor. The telescope is the great-granddaddy of all of these wondrous machines. It was the first scientific tool ever invented for expanding our view of the heavens, and it forever changed the way scientists looked at nature. The telescope showed that ordinary observers could see things of which no one had ever dreamed. Today's telescopes have brought a golden age of exploration, the likes of which have not been seen since the discovery of the New World five hundred years ago.

Astronomy is the study of everything in the universe that lies beyond our tiny planet Earth. The universe is full of all types of objects: stars, galaxies, moons, planets, and comets, to name just a few. These objects didn't always exist. There had to be a beginning, and everything in space may someday come to an end. This means the universe is changing over time. Stars explode, galaxies collide, asteroids zip menacingly by Earth, and strange objects called black holes devour stars. Telescopes are used to probe these mysteries. More than any other single scientific instrument, the telescope is used to unlock timeless questions: Where did Earth and the Sun come from? Are there planets around other stars? How did the universe begin? When will it end? Could there be intelligent life in space? The answers to these questions could fundamentally change the way we think about ourselves and our place in nature.

This book explores the tremendous imagination and inventiveness that scientists and engineers have used to build larger and more powerful telescopes. Telescopes are glass and steel giants that must be built with the strength of a bridge but must work as precisely as a fine watch. Today they have evolved to become unimaginably accurate, computer-powered machines for processing starlight from long ago and far away. Previous generations have expressed their awe of the universe by building great monuments, pyramids, and cathedrals. Today's giant telescopes are scientific monuments to our curiosity about the infinite universe.

Right: This glowing cloud is a giant starbirth region (nebula NGC 604) in the neighboring galaxy M33, with more than 200 massive, young stars in its heart. Image from Hubble Space Telescope. *Courtesy of NASA.*

Below: This diagram shows a telescope with about a 5-foot (150-cm) mirror similar to that which was installed on Mt. Palomar in California. The parts have been labeled for reference.

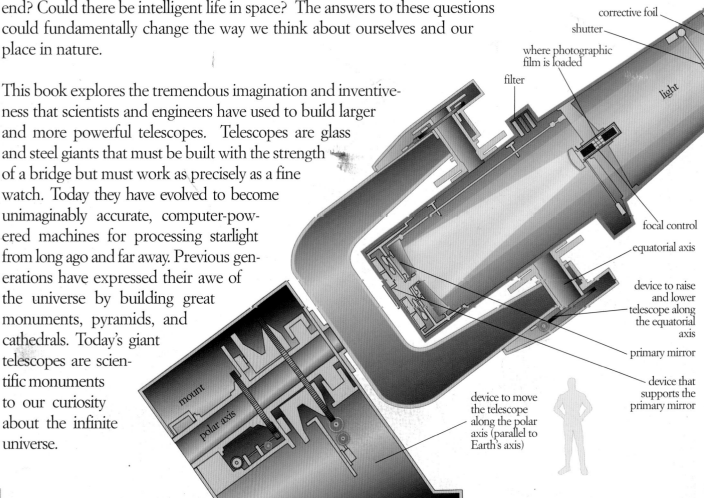

corrective foil
shutter
where photographic film is loaded
filter
light
focal control
equatorial axis
device to raise and lower telescope along the equatorial axis
primary mirror
device that supports the primary mirror
device to move the telescope along the polar axis (parallel to Earth's axis)
mount
polar axis

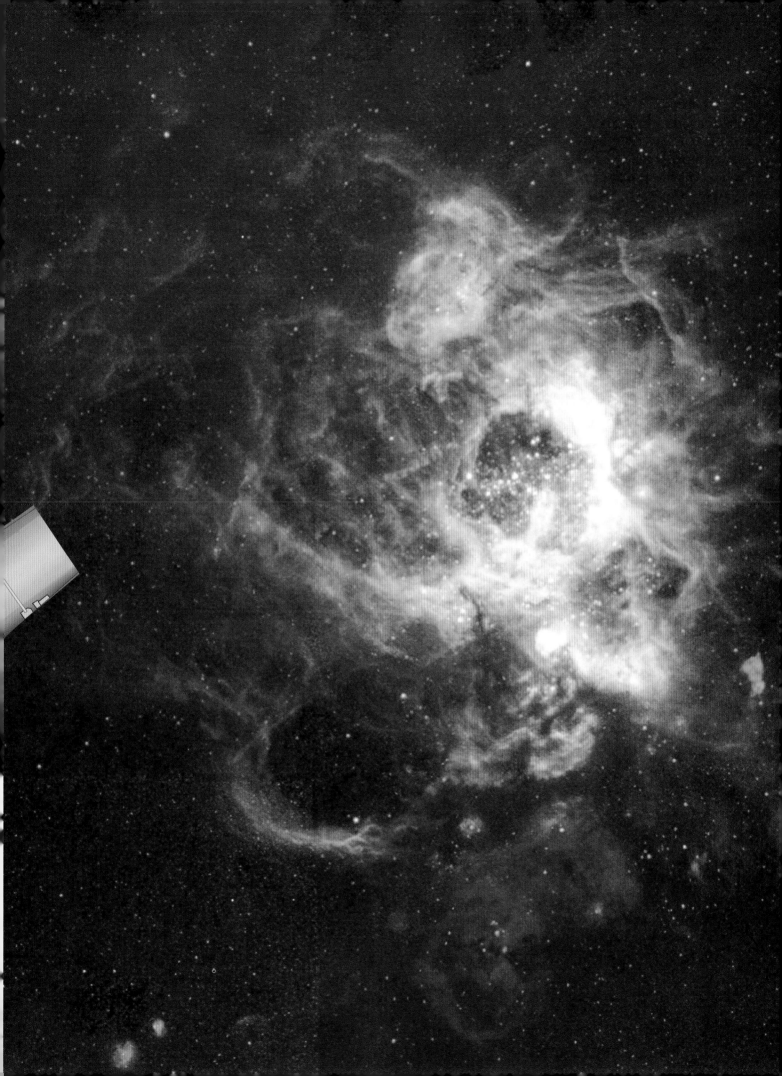

Looking at Light

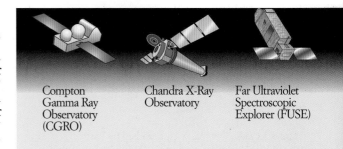

A telescope collects and concentrates light, allowing distant and faint objects to be seen as if they were much closer to us. The word telescope, taken from the Greek word *teleskop,* means "to see far." Unlike other sciences, astronomers cannot directly touch the objects they study. A biologist can physically probe the workings of a cell, a geologist can break apart rocks, and a paleontologist can unearth dinosaur bones that have been preserved for eons. We have sent space probes to the planets, but the stars, nebulae, and galaxies are so distant that they cannot be visited. The only way they can be studied is by the nature of their light.

How Light Works

The light that a telescope collects can be used to make pictures of planets, stars, and galaxies, or it can be divided into a rainbow of colors, called the spectrum, that carries information about different types of objects in the universe. Before astronomers can begin to understand the universe, they must understand the nature of light. Picture what happens when you throw a stone into a pond. Waves ripple across the pond in all directions, carrying the energy released by the stone's impact. Think of light as ripples of energy from stars. Scientists talk about light as having a wavelength that is a measure of the distance between each wave of energy. Waves on an ocean may be feet (m) apart, but waves of light are only about 1/10,000 of an inch (2.54 cm) apart! Blue light has shorter wavelengths than does red light, so the wavelength of light also tells us something about color. Stars look white because they emit all the colors of the rainbow, but a star's true color can be slightly reddish or bluish, depending on its temperature and the speed at which it's moving through space.

The speed and the direction of light can be controlled in various ways. Its speed and direction change when it passes through a transparent medium, such as glass. This is a process called refraction. Light waves also can bounce off surfaces and be sent in a different direction. This is called reflection. A mirror's shiny surface is the best reflector of light. Light also can be split, or separated, into all the separate colors that make up white light. A glass prism does this by bending different colors of light. The droplets of water in the atmosphere behave like a microscopic prism to make a rainbow. The very fine, invisible grooves in a compact disc (CD) also split apart light into a rainbow of colors. This is called diffraction.

Below: Earth's atmosphere is denser closer to sea level. The denser the atmosphere is the more it refracts light. As starlight passes through, it bends and the star appears higher on the horizon than it actually is.

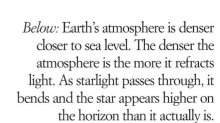

	Where light of star bends in the atmosphere
A	Angle of refraction
☆	Apparent position
★	Real position
z	Point of incident
	Atmosphere

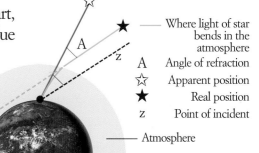

Compton Gamma Ray Observatory (CGRO)

Chandra X-Ray Observatory

Far Ultraviolet Spectroscopic Explorer (FUSE)

| 0.0001nm | 0.001nm | 0.01nm | 0.1nm | 1nm |

gamma rays   X rays

INVISIBLE LIGHT

In 1800, the British scientist and astronomer Sir William Herschel was amazed to discover that he could measure "invisible light" coming from a prism. Using a thermometer, he found that the temperatures of the colors in sunlight increased from the blue to the red part of the spectrum. Herschel decided to measure the temperature just beyond the red portion of the spectrum, in a region that seemed to have no sunlight. To his surprise, he found this region had the highest temperature of all! It was eventually called infrared radiation. Herschel's discovery was the first time that someone proved there are forms of light that we cannot see.

Scientists eventually realized that light is really only a small part of a much broader range of energies in the universe, called the electromagnetic spectrum. This spectrum is a flood of radiation produced by the constant jiggling and colliding of atoms, the basic building blocks of matter. This electromagnetic radiation includes radio waves, microwaves, infrared light, visible light, ultraviolet light, X rays, and gamma rays.

Our atmosphere only allows light, radio waves, and some infrared radiation to travel to Earth's surface. This is good because other forms of radiation are harmful to us. To see other radiation, astronomers must launch telescopes into space beyond our atmosphere. Different types of telescopes detect electromagnetic radiation from a variety of objects in space. Different objects give off different kinds of radiation. Stars radiate mostly visible light. Planets shine in infrared light. Black holes glow in X-ray light. Gas clouds shine in radio light. Because of this, telescopes come in a wide variety of shapes and sizes. Their size and appearance depend on the type of radiation they were designed to detect.

Left, top: The glass with a pencil in it shows how light bends. This shows refraction of light.

Below: These diagrams show how reflective (top) and a refractive (bottom) telescopes work.

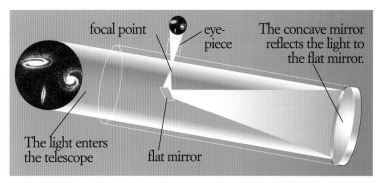

focal point   eyepiece   The concave mirror reflects the light to the flat mirror.

The light enters the telescope   flat mirror

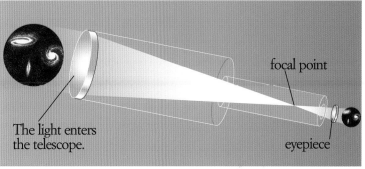

The light enters the telescope.   focal point   eyepiece

Below: This chart shows the different types of light, based on wavelength, and the different types of instruments that detect them.

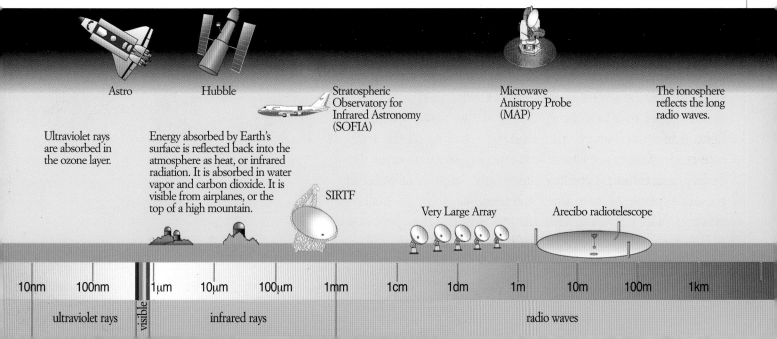

Astro   Hubble   Stratospheric Observatory for Infrared Astronomy (SOFIA)   Microwave Anistropy Probe (MAP)   The ionosphere reflects the long radio waves.

Ultraviolet rays are absorbed in the ozone layer.   Energy absorbed by Earth's surface is reflected back into the atmosphere as heat, or infrared radiation. It is absorbed in water vapor and carbon dioxide. It is visible from airplanes, or the top of a high mountain.   SIRTF   Very Large Array   Arecibo radiotelescope

10nm	100nm	1µm	10µm	100µm	1mm	1cm	1dm	1m	10m	100m	1km

ultraviolet rays   visible   infrared rays   radio waves

Giant Eye on the Sky

In some ways, a telescope is simply a scaled-up version of the eye. Like the eye, a basic telescope uses a lens to collect light. The lens bends incoming light. The hamburger-bun, or convex, shape of the lens bends light at the edge of the lens at a greater angle than the light coming through the center so that all the beams arrive at a point or a focus at the back of the eye. The retina collects the light and converts it to electronic signals that are transmitted to the vision centers of the brain.

The first telescopes used glass lenses shaped just like the eye's, but much bigger, to bend faint starlight and to bring it to a focus, where all the light beams come together. It's like trying to arrange a meeting where people from all parts of a town travel to the center at exactly the same moment. The larger the lens the more light it can collect. The human eye's lens is only 1/5 of an inch (0.5 cm) across. A glass lens 1 inch (2.5 cm) across has twenty-five times as much surface area as the eye, so it collects twenty-five times as much light. Mirrors also can be shaped to capture light and to bring it to a focus. The biggest telescopic mirrors sparkle with the sensitivity of several hundred million human eyes working together!

HOW ASTRONOMERS USE TELESCOPES

Much of astronomy is simply the skill of looking. Throughout the history of astronomy, research has been done by directly viewing celestial objects through a telescope's eyepiece. The eyepiece provides a magnified image of the light that has been brought to a focus. Early astronomers spent many hours peering through the eyepiece of a telescope and making sketches of what they saw. The earliest observations were simply an inventory of everything of a certain size or brightness that could be seen through a telescope. Repeated observations over time allowed astronomers to keep track of changes in the universe such as the passage of a comet, the pulsation of a star, or the weather on other planets. Today electronic cameras record images in stunning color. Telescopes today are often used to make pictures. These images are used to

Right: This diagram shows the VLT Interferometer. This telescope combines the information collected by four large and two auxiliary telescopes. Each tries to capture different parts of the same light wave arriving from space. The beams from the telescopes must be lined up so each light wave matches up with its other portion as though one huge telescope (which would be impossible to actually create) has collected the information.

SPECTROSCOPY

In spectroscopy light from a celestial object is carried through a narrow slit and then spread out into a rainbow of color. A spectroscope precisely measures the brightness of different colors across the rainbow spectrum. A spectroscope's design can either use the principles of refraction (in a prism) or diffraction (in a finely etched mirror).

Diagram A: A prism is one way to split light by refraction. The light, made of varying wavelengths, is refracted, or bent, at different angles onto the CCD.
Diagram B: In a similar fashion to that of a prism, a reflective grating, (like the

reflective surface of a CD-ROM) also refracts the light and reflects it against the CCD or light sensor as individual waves. The ridges in the reflective grating cause the different wavelengths of light to bounce off at different angles.

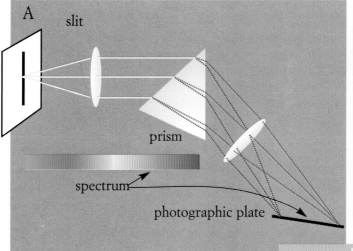

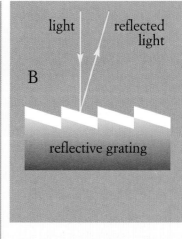

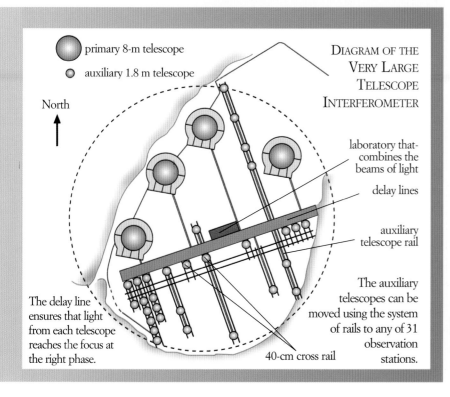

DIAGRAM OF THE VERY LARGE TELESCOPE INTERFEROMETER

primary 8-m telescope
auxiliary 1.8 m telescope

North

laboratory that combines the beams of light

delay lines

auxiliary telescope rail

The auxiliary telescopes can be moved using the system of rails to any of 31 observation stations.

The delay line ensures that light from each telescope reaches the focus at the right phase.

40-cm cross rail

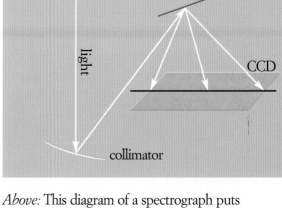

Above: This diagram of a spectrograph puts together what we learned in Diagrams A and B. The light of a star filters through the slit and reaches the lens. The lens focuses the light onto the reflective grating, which then separates the light waves. The CCD developer reads the light and creates a picture.

categorize the appearance, the shape, and the color of deep-sky objects such as a galaxy, a nebula, or a comet.

Besides providing images, the light collected by a telescope is divided into its colors through a process called spectroscopy. This powerful technique, which uses a finely etched mirror called a diffraction grating, essentially "decodes" starlight to yield information about an object's temperature, motion, distance, and chemical composition.

Left page, top right: This is the observatory in Hven, Denmark, where the great Danish astronomer Tycho Brahe made the observations that would, in turn, allow Johannes Kepler to come up with his famous laws about the motion of the planets.

Left, bottom: This is a huge telescope mirror blank and the team that has worked to create it.

From Simple Beginnings

Dutch eyeglass maker Hans Lippershey invented the first telescope in the year 1608. He discovered that by simply peering through a pair of glass lenses held in front of each other, a distant object appeared to be much closer. Despite attempts to keep it a secret, news of the telescope's invention spread rapidly through Europe.

In 1609, the Italian scientist Galileo Galilei used a homemade telescope that made objects appear thirty times closer. To his amazement, he could see mountains and valleys on the Moon. He observed four moons orbiting the planet Jupiter, saw that the Milky Way galaxy was made up of countless stars, and saw dark spots on the Sun. Almost overnight, the telescope had revolutionized our view of the universe.

BIG MIRRORS REPLACE LENSES

Telescope technology took another giant leap forward in 1688, when scientist Sir Isaac Newton built a completely different type of telescope. Instead of using lenses, which magnified light through refraction, he used a slightly curved mirror to collect light through reflection. Newton's mirror was only 1.5 inches (3.8 cm) across, but it revolutionized astronomy. His invention paved the way for much larger mirrors to be built. Mirrors were extremely lightweight compared to lenses and were far more powerful because they collected more starlight.

Above: Galileo Galilei, the father of modern astronomy, with one of his telescopes, which can be seen at the Museum of the History of Science in Florence, Italy.

In the 1700s, Sir William Herschel, a British astronomer, was the next to push telescope size to new heights, constructing telescopes as big as 48 inches (1.2 m) in diameter and 40 feet (12 m) in length. Then in the 1800s, scientist William Parsons built a 72-inch (1.8-m), reflecting telescope with a mirror that weighed 3 tons (2.7 t). The telescope tube was 58 feet (20 m) long.

TELESCOPES GO THROUGH A GROWTH SPURT

The twentieth century saw an explosive growth in telescope size. Telescope mirrors doubled in diameter every thirty-five years. In 1928, astronomers undertook one of the greatest engineering achievements of modern science. With a six-million-dollar grant from the Rockefeller Foundation, they spent the next twenty years building the 200-inch (5-m) mirror for the Hale Telescope located on Mount Palomar in California. When it went into operation in 1948, it stood seven stories tall and consisted of at least 250,000 specially-designed parts. The Hale Telescope remained the best in the world for nearly half a century. To make telescopes any larger using conventional design, would also mean making mirrors thicker. The weight of such a mirror, more than 14 tons (12.7 t), would make it extremely difficult to move. New engineering breakthroughs would be needed first—and these were unimaginable in 1948.

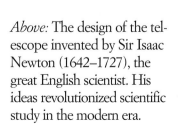

Above: The design of the telescope invented by Sir Isaac Newton (1642–1727), the great English scientist. His ideas revolutionized scientific study in the modern era.

DIAGRAM OF HOW THE NEWTONIAN REFLECTIVE TELESCOPE WORKS

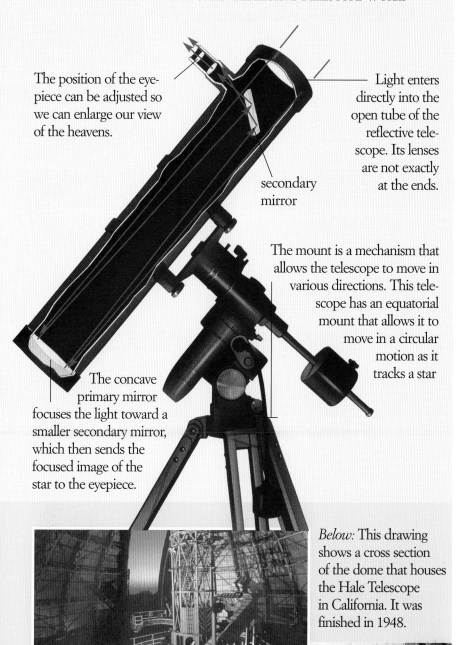

The position of the eyepiece can be adjusted so we can enlarge our view of the heavens.

Light enters directly into the open tube of the reflective telescope. Its lenses are not exactly at the ends.

secondary mirror

The mount is a mechanism that allows the telescope to move in various directions. This telescope has an equatorial mount that allows it to move in a circular motion as it tracks a star

The concave primary mirror focuses the light toward a smaller secondary mirror, which then sends the focused image of the star to the eyepiece.

Below: This drawing shows a cross section of the dome that houses the Hale Telescope in California. It was finished in 1948.

Above: The great, 100-inch (2.5 m) telescope on Mount Wilson in California allowed Edwin Hubble to discover that the Milky Way was just one of many galaxies and that the universe is expanding.

VARIATIONS OF THE NEWTONIAN TELESCOPE

The Cassegrain system—named after the French physicist Cassegrain who described it in 1672—uses a little secondary mirror mounted closer to the focal point of the primary mirror. The light entering the telescope bounces off the primary mirror to the small mirror and is reflected back out through the eyepiece. This effect is called folded optics, which increases the focal length of an instrument, allowing it to see objects that are farther away.

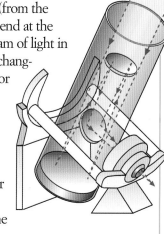

CASSEGRAIN

The coudé diagram (from the French *couder*, "to bend at the elbow") aims the beam of light in a fixed direction by changing the angle of one or more adjustable secondary mirrors. This means that a person does not need to change position to view an object. He or she just adjusts the mirror to focus on the desired object.

COUDÉ

Edwin Hubble

Advances in Telescope Technology

On October 7, 1958, the former Soviet Union launched the first artificial satellite, named *Sputnik,* into orbit around Earth. The soccer-ball-sized *Sputnik* launched a technological competition between the United States and the Soviets called the space race, which triggered a chain of events leading to the development of powerful new telescopes. Some of these advances included miniature electronics, the development of mirrors with crystal-clear views, and the use of Charge-Coupled Devices (CCDs) instead of film. CCDs have a number of advantages over film. They are much more sensitive to light and display excellent contrasts, which means they can see bright objects near faint objects. The image is automatically recorded in digital form, so it can be enhanced by a computer and stored. CCDs made telescopes more powerful without increasing their size.

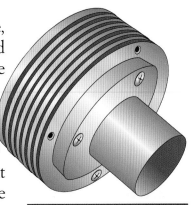

BREAKTHROUGHS IN TELESCOPE SIZE

By the 1980s, astronomers had done just about everything they could using the best CCD cameras and the biggest telescopes of the time. Astronomers were still "light-starved," which meant they needed even bigger mirrors than in the 200-inch (5-m) Hale. This called for engineering imagination and innovation. Computers again came to the rescue, offering previously unimagined possibilities.

One idea was to make very thin mirrors that would be lighter and that could be moved with greater ease. However, this would require computer control to keep a mirror from changing shape, which could ruin observations. This was first tried on the European Southern Observatory's (ESO's) New Technology Telescope (NTT) built in 1988. In 1998, its successor, ESO's Very Large Telescope (VLT), opened and remains one of the best observatories today.

Above: The CCD is more efficient and sensitive to light than a photographic plate.

Below: A mirror is about to be cast using the spin-cast method. This method saves time because the mirror is cast very close to its exact shape.

An even more radical idea was to assemble a gigantic mirror from individual mirror pieces like the compound eye of an insect. This again required computer control to make the segmented mirror provide the same image quality as one single, gigantic piece of glass. This led to the building of the pioneer for all future giant telescopes, the revolutionary Keck Telescope, which opened in 1990. That year also saw the launch of the Hubble Space Telescope, which began the era of putting major telescopes in space.

A telescope can be thought of as a "light bucket." The bigger the telescope, the more efficiently it can collect light, just as a big bucket collects more rainwater than does a small cup. The

largest telescopes typically can detect objects that are more than one billionth the brightness of the faintest star seen by the human eye. If your eye were as sensitive, you would be able to see the glow of a firefly halfway around the world. Having a bright image is not the only answer. The telescope's view must be sharp, too. To be useful, a telescope must be able to see very fine detail in distant objects. In theory, the bigger the mirror, the sharper the image. However, even the biggest telescope imaginable must deal with the fact that the atmosphere blurs starlight. It's like looking at the sky from the bottom of a swimming pool. That is why stars appear to twinkle at night.

Without additional technology, the biggest ground-based telescope cannot provide a sharper image than what can be seen through a moderate-size telescope that you can buy in a store. However, computers allow ground-based telescopes to sharpen their images by controlling tiny, flexible mirrors that subtract the atmosphere's blurring effect by keeping track of ever-changing distortions in the atmosphere. This is called active optics (see page 22).

Top Right: This is a Hubble Space Telescope image of Saturn. *Courtesy of NASA.*

Bottom Right: Mirror segments in the Keck Telescope are anchored to a motorized support structure.

Telescope Design

When designing a telescope, engineers must take into account the size of the mirror, the telescope structure, and the way the entire unit, or assembly, will move. A weak link in the system will hurt the telescope's entire performance. Though a telescope has many mirrors and optical elements, the key piece is the primary mirror. Its design determines how the rest of the telescope will be built.

The light captured by the primary mirror must be sent to cameras and other instruments. Usually the beam bounces off the primary mirror and travels back up the tube to a much smaller secondary mirror. Like the primary mirror, the secondary mirror may be controlled by a computer to sharpen the image further. Once the beam bounces off the secondary mirror, it travels back down the tube and passes through a hole in the center of the primary mirror. This zigzag path through a telescope is called folded optics, because the light path bends back onto itself. Behind the primary mirror, the beam may bounce off a third, correcting mirror until it finally comes to a focus where the instruments that record the image are. All the pieces must be connected to each other in a cage-like structure called the optical telescope assembly. The individual pieces must stay at exactly the same distance from each other even though the telescope moves throughout the night.

This diagram shows how a telescope with folded optics collects and focuses light.

secondary mirror | primary mirror | focus

Today's modern telescope mirror needs to be big to collect a lot of light, but it can't be so heavy that it sags under its own weight or bends when it moves. It cannot change shape due to wind or temperature extremes common to the mountain top location of most observatories. This would distort the images the mirror receives or pull them out of focus. A telescope mirror cannot be flat. It must be slightly curved, like a very shallow bowl.

Below: The primary mirror is the key to telescope design. This is one of 32 segments of glass before it was shaped and polished to become the Keck Telescope mirror.

This shape is called concave. The idea is that no matter where a particle of light hits the mirror, it will be reflected to a point called the focus.

The early telescope shape was a relatively simple curve, basically a section of a sphere. If you sliced a coconut down the middle, both bowl-shaped halves would be sections of a sphere. A more precise shape is a special curve called a parabola. One challenge for designers is that the bigger a parabolic mirror the longer the reflected light must travel before it comes to a focus. This distance is called focal length.

A telescope mirror bigger than the 200-inch (5-m) Hale Telescope would need an extremely long and heavy tube to carry the rays of light to the secondary mirror. This in turn would mean a large, heavy telescope and a huge, expensive dome. Because computers can guide the shaping of the mirror, a much more complicated, deeper curve, called a hyperbola, can be made. This would be impossible to do without the help of computers. Such mirror surfaces are so precise that they make it possible to build telescopes with shorter focal lengths. This makes the telescope tube shorter and lighter. A light structure allows for a larger telescope to be made and gives the telescope a wider view of the heavens.

ACTIVE MIRRORS

One of the advances in telescope design allows very thin mirrors to be constructed. Active optics (see page 17) are used to help the mirror keep its shape. This diagram shows the active optics of the Very Large Telescope (VLT). The active optics are indicated by the green arrows. A computer makes tiny adjustments to the curvature of the mirror, by pushing one of the plungers supporting the mirror.

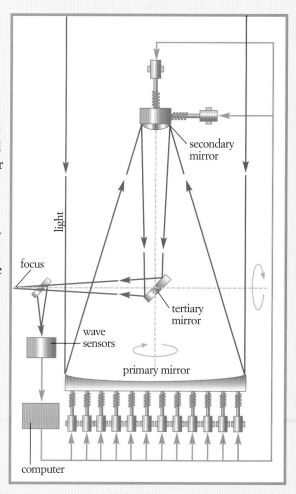

LIQUID MIRRORS

NASA's 118-inch (3-m) Liquid Mirror Telescope is used to study debris in space. The inexpensive telescope uses 3.7 gallons (14 l) of mercury and spins constantly. The liquid mercury sits in a dish that is an almost exact parabaloid shape, which is spin cast. Air-bearings are used to keep vibrations at a minimum as the dish is spinning. This allows for a clearer picture of the object being viewed.

Right: This is a diagram of a typical liquid mirror.

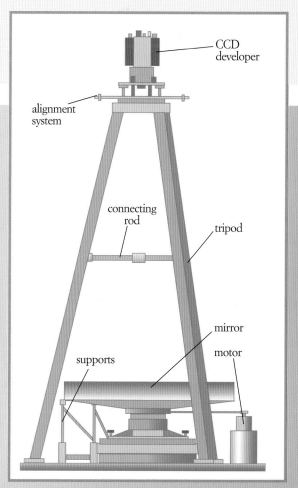

The Mirror

Casting the Mirror

Glass is the best material for telescope mirrors. It is rigid, strong, relatively inexpensive, and can be polished to be extremely smooth. A thin coating of silver or aluminum is applied to make the polished glass into a mirror. Telescope mirrors must be cast from special molten, or liquid, glass that will not significantly expand or contract in response to temperature once it cools and hardens.

Once the glass is cast and hardened, it resembles a giant hockey puck. It is called a mirror blank, because it still has to be polished to a curved shape. Mirror blanks used to be more than 1 foot (30 cm) thick. They were cast so that the back had a honeycomb shape, which lowered the weight of the mirror. Once the molten glass is cast as a mirror blank, it must cool slowly to avoid cracking. The first mirror cast for the mighty Hale Telescope cracked after one year of cooling. A second mirror had to be made.

Above: These people are getting ready to add the aluminum coating to a mirror blank.

Left: Glass chunks are being placed in a honeycomb mold. This will later be placed in an oven and will be spun into a parabola shape.

Far Right: This is a mirror blank before it has been ground and polished.

Below: Technicians are cleaning Hale's 200-inch (5-m) mirror.

Mirror Grinding and Polishing

The biggest challenge comes next. The flat mirror blank's surface must be ground to precisely the right shape. For a long time, this was done by hand. Grinding the glass for the Hale Telescope's mirror took thirteen years! Opticians ground away 7 tons (6.3 t) of powdered glass. Today engineers use a computer-controlled grinder. It rubs a mudlike mixture of water and powder across the glass, slowly reshaping it from a flat surface into a slightly curved one.

Once the surface of the mirror has the right curved shape, it must be buffed to incredible smoothness. The mirror must be smooth to within 1/100 the thickness of a human hair. A mirror is made incredibly smooth with a computerized polishing machine that looks like a robotic, circular floor sander. Engineers also have developed a new process in which a machine fires a beam of atoms at the mirror's surface. These tiny atomic "bullets" knock the smallest irregularities off the surface of the mirror.

New Casting Techniques Simplify Grinding

It takes years to reshape carefully a mirror from a glass slab to a shallow, precise bowl shape. What if the mirror could be cast in the right shape when the molten glass is first poured? That's the idea behind a new technique called spin-casting. During spin casting, the mirror blank is spun on a huge carousel while the glass is still molten. The rotation moves some of the glass toward the edge of the spinning container, like when you stir water in a bowl. The molten glass—or water—will make a shape called a paraboloide. The advantage is that, after it cools, a mirror does not have to be ground to remove excess glass. It is already very close to its exact shape. This saves a lot of time.

This spin-casting technique was pioneered at the University of Arizona's Steward Observatory Mirror Lab by astronomer Roger Angel. He built ovens big enough to cast mirrors up to 300 inches (8 m) across. Solid pieces of glass are arranged in a circular form like an oversized cake pan. The glass is heated until it flows like molten wax into honeycomb molds. After five days—when the temperature has reached 2,100°F (1,148°C)—the heat is turned down and the mirror spends many weeks in a controlled cooldown to avoid cracking.

Tuning Up Telescopes

The immense, fragile mirror at the heart of a telescope takes constant maintenance. At some observatories, technicians wash the mirror once or twice a year, because it is exposed to the elements almost every night and gets dirty. They use regular soap, water, and natural ocean sponges to clean it. The aluminum on the mirror has to be replaced every few years, because oxygen in the atmosphere corrodes it.

When the Hale Telescope mirror was recently refurbished, technicians found that water droplets combined with brush-fire ash had eaten through the ultrathin layer of reflective aluminum. They even found a dead bug!

Coating the Mirror

To create the reflective surface of a telescope mirror, technicians place a very thin coat of aluminum (or silver) on the glass. To accomplish this, the blank is placed inside a vacuum chamber, where most of the air is pumped out. Next filaments coated with 1 ounce (28 g) of aluminum are heated. As the aluminum heats up, its atoms fly across the chamber and settle on the blank's surface. The vacuum is needed so that there aren't air molecules bouncing around to block the aluminum from forming an extremely thin, smooth coat on the glass.

Telescope Innovations

New casting and polishing techniques are now allowing engineers to make extremely thin mirrors called meniscus mirrors. A thin piece of glass solves two problems. It reduces the mirror's weight and it keeps the mirror from retaining heat. However, a thin mirror also can be too flexible to work properly. The mirror can sag under the pull of gravity and can be moved out of position by wind.

Engineers have solved this problem by putting many tiny pistons, called servo-mechanical actuators, behind the meniscus mirrors. Controlled by computer, the actuators adjust the shape of the mirror four times a second. This technique is called active optics (see page 17). Any slight deviations in the mirror's curve send commands to the actuators to push and to pull sections of the mirror by a distance that is no more than 1/10,000 the thickness of a human hair!

Top: Large telescopes have been limited in size because they need to be transported to mountaintop observatories on roads.

Bottom: Michael Best measures hexagonal blanks made of Ultra-Low Expansion glass. They will be used to make one large mirror for the Japanese National Telescope on Mauna Kea in Hawaii.

A 300-inch (7.6-m) mirror—the size of a backyard swimming pool—is probably the limit for the size of single big mirrors. Larger ones would take many more actuators and would take longer to cool to operating temperature at night. A mirror 300 inches (7.6 m) across is also the biggest mirror that can be transported on highways—not to mention the narrow, winding roads that lead to mountaintop observatories.

In the early 1980s, astronomer Jerry Nelson of the University of California at Berkeley proposed building a telescope that would use many smaller mirrors—like covering a floor with individual tiles—rather than one giant, mirrored sheet. His thinking was that the mirrors would be lighter and cheaper to grind. They would be linked together through a computer-controlled system that would keep the mirrors perfectly aligned. Nelson's design called for mass-producing thirty-six, 70-inch-wide (1.8-m-wide) hexagonal mirrors that, when assembled, would form a perfect parabola. This design made it easier to transport the glass, which was cast in Germany, polished in California and Massachusetts, and shipped to Hawaii by Federal Express!

Unlike floor tiles, where each piece is exactly the same shape, the mirror pieces are more like a jigsaw puzzle in which no two pieces are exactly alike. Imagine a very shallow bowl. If you broke it apart, each piece would have a curve slightly different from all the other pieces, depending on their distance from the bowl's center. If the pieces were glued back together, the dish would regain its perfect shape, even though each piece would be imperfect.

Grinding and polishing each blank to its own unique shape was a difficult task. Nelson and his colleagues used a technique called stress polishing. Each blank was warped through forces applied to handles attached to the bottom. Each blank was then ground and polished to the shape of a normal mirror. When technicians let go of the handles, the blanks sprang back to their original shapes.

MOVING THE TELESCOPE

A large telescope is a mammoth, heavy, yet delicate construction. The biggest telescopes today weigh nearly 300 tons (272 t)! One of the biggest challenges facing engineers is how to make the entire massive structure move smoothly and precisely. The telescope must be mounted so that the mirror assembly can be pivoted to easily track the stars. Earth's axis points in the direction of the star Polaris, also called the North Star. A telescope's rotation axis also must point to the North Star. This is easy for backyard, amateur telescopes, but it is tough for large telescopes. The telescope slowly pivoting about its axis causes enormous stresses that can only be overcome by making the telescope massive and very expensive.

A much simpler way to move a telescope is to have the telescope tube pivot up and down and rotate on a platform like a carousel. This is the way a large artillery gun is aimed. The trouble is that the telescope has to tilt slightly every few moments to keep track of a star. This would be hard to do by hand. Thanks to computers, this complex motion of a telescope can be easily controlled. Today all big telescopes have mounts like artillery guns have. This opened the door for building much larger and relatively lightweight telescopes.

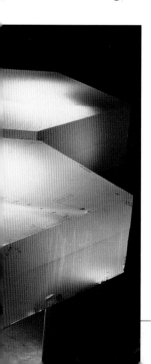

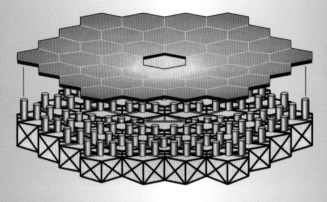

Segmented mirrors, like the one Jerry Nelson proposed, incorporate many small, thin mirrors, which are easier to build and to support than a single large mirror. Motorized controllers keep the segments aligned so that they form a single image.

Meniscus mirrors are another innovation that allows for larger mirror sizes. These mirrors are solid but too thin to support their own weight. Mechanical actuators adjust the mirrors, so that they are always bent to the correct shape.

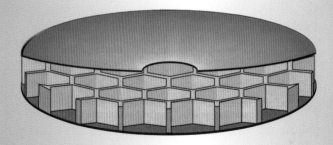

Honeycomb mirrors consist of a thin reflective surface atop glass honeycomb structures. These mirrors are stiff but very light because each cell of the honeycomb is filled with air rather than being a solid piece of glass.

A Sharper View

Despite the growth of telescope size, astronomers still were frustrated by the lack of image sharpness. When astronomers looked at the image of a single, twinkling star, they realized they were really looking at an image that had been scattered and blurred by the turbulent atmosphere. This happens because light travels through pockets of air in the atmosphere that act like lenses by bending the light. This makes the light zigzag through the atmosphere and appear to twinkle.

Astronomers had to figure out how to reassemble a star back into one clear image just before it finished its trip through the telescope. They thought a small "rubber mirror" could collect the "shimmering" image of a star and could put it back together.

This system is called adaptive optics. The key to it is a special light sensor that rapidly keeps track of a star's moving light. At least twenty times every second, the sensor sends commands to tiny actuators behind the mirror. The actuators bend the mirror in exactly the opposite direction of the distortion. This puts the star's image back together, concentrating the light into a small point rather than into a smeared blob.

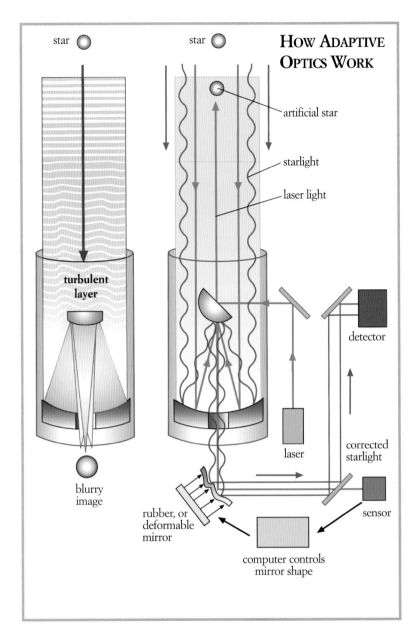

How Adaptive Optics Work

star · star · artificial star · starlight · laser light · turbulent layer · detector · blurry image · rubber, or deformable mirror · laser · corrected starlight · sensor · computer controls mirror shape

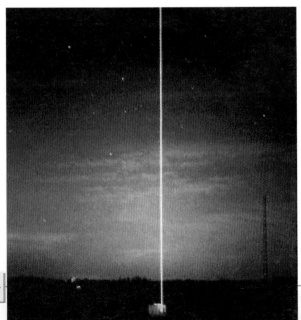

HUMANMADE STARS

To work successfully, adaptive optics systems need a relatively bright star in the telescope's view. The problem is that bright stars are not always near the object that a telescope needs to observe. Astronomers came up with a way to make an artificial star that could be placed anywhere in the sky. To do this, a laser is fired more than one thousand times per second at a thin layer of atmosphere 55 miles (88.5 km) up. The reflected laser beam comes back to the telescope through the same atmospheric cells that are distorting the starlight, so the laser beam smears in the same way. This gives the sensors the information they need to take the smear out of the real starlight.

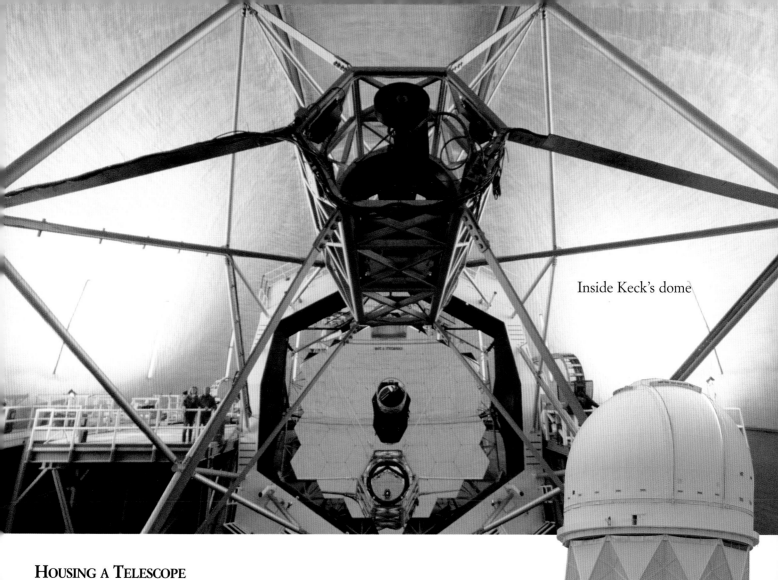

Inside Keck's dome

HOUSING A TELESCOPE

When people think of telescopes, they often think of the buildings in which they are housed. The classic image is of a circular building with a magnificent, dome-shaped roof. The dome has a door that closes to protect the telescope from rain. The dome must also rotate in a full circle. This can get very expensive for huge telescopes. Engineers who built the New Technology Telescope came up with a clever approach that allows the entire building to rotate like a carousel. This eliminates the weight and the complexity of a separate dome that has to be disconnected from the base of the building so that it can rotate on its own special track. More recent domes were designed to allow the outside air to flow easily around the dome to reduce air turbulence that would blur starlight. One of the most aerodynamic observatories is the dome for the 158-inch (4-m) Mayall Telescope, at Kitt Peak in Arizona.

When astronomers began using CCD detectors, they became aware of other dome problems. The CCD exposures revealed that there was turbulence inside the dome. Some modern domes are ventilated by flaps that blow air across the telescope mirror. This keeps rising air from collecting just above the telescope's surface—as heat does on a hot asphalt road. Motors in the dome are cooled by water to prevent heat from collecting inside the building. Electronics boxes located on the telescope are insulated and cooled. The building, concrete platforms, and parking lots around the telescope are painted bright white to reflect away most of the sunlight, reducing the amount of heat that builds up during the day.

Above: Kitt Peak's aerodynamic Mayall Telescope stands about 7,000 feet (2,134 m) above sea level.

Far Left: A laser beam is fired near a celestial object that an atronomer wants to observe.

The Hubble Space Telescope

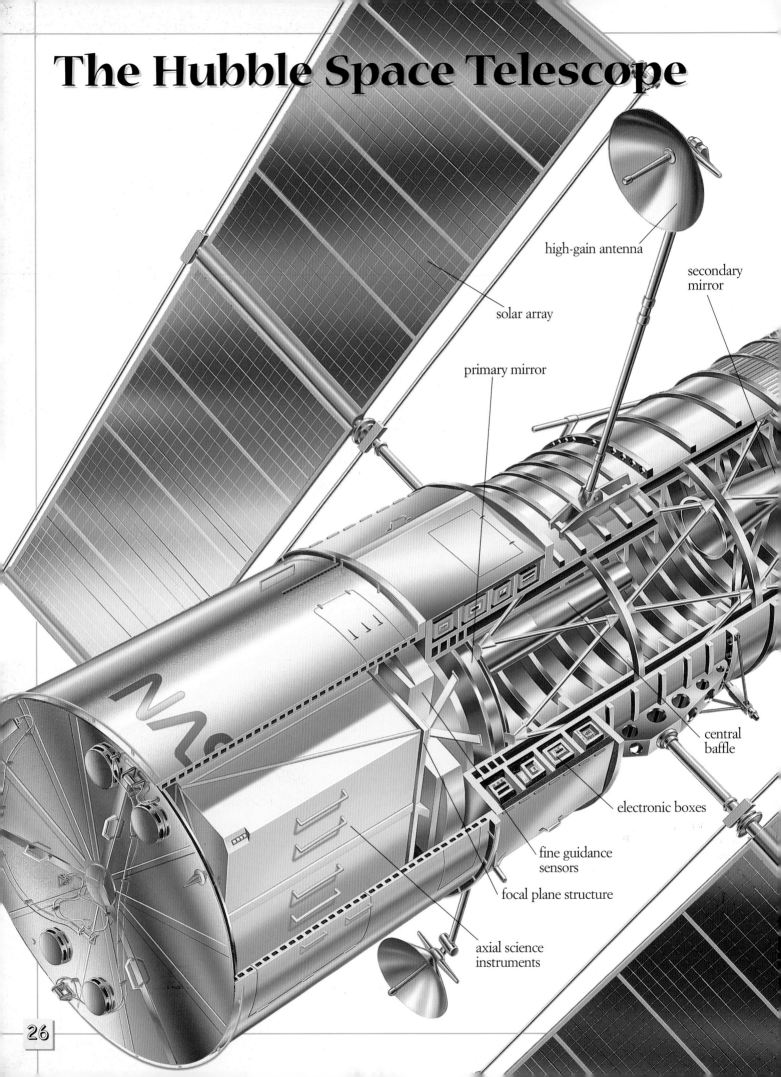

high-gain antenna

secondary mirror

solar array

primary mirror

central baffle

electronic boxes

fine guidance sensors

focal plane structure

axial science instruments

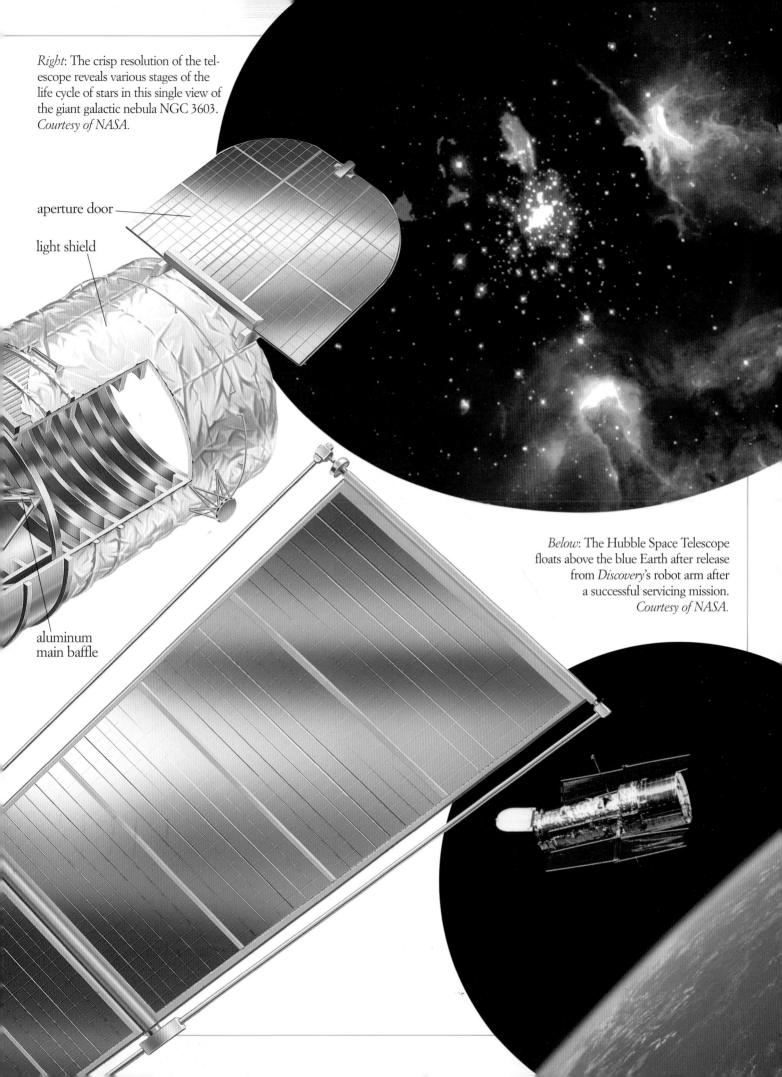

Right: The crisp resolution of the telescope reveals various stages of the life cycle of stars in this single view of the giant galactic nebula NGC 3603. *Courtesy of NASA.*

aperture door

light shield

aluminum main baffle

Below: The Hubble Space Telescope floats above the blue Earth after release from *Discovery*'s robot arm after a successful servicing mission. *Courtesy of NASA.*

The Hubble Space Telescope Structure

The Hubble Space Telescope will long be remembered as the telescope that opened a revolutionary new eye on the universe, revealing dazzling views of stars and galaxies never before imagined. The Hubble, named after astronomer Edwin Powell Hubble, is the first major infrared-optical-ultraviolet telescope to be placed into orbit around Earth. Its unique vantage point has allowed us to gain information once out of reach. This includes Hubble's study of deep fields in the northern and the southern hemispheres of the sky. Deep fields are areas of space so remote, we have never been able to see them before.

The heart of the telescope is a 94.5-inch (2.4-m) mirror. It is one of the smoothest optical mirrors ever polished and weighs about 1,800 pounds (816.5 kg). The Hubble mirror is assembled like a sandwich. The mirror is only 3 inches (7.6 cm) thick. It is connected to an egg-crate-shaped structure and a back plate of more glass (see diagram below). Unlike ground-based telescopes, astronomers cannot look through Hubble's lens to see the universe. Instead, Hubble's electronic instruments are the astronomers' eyes. The telescope's instruments include cameras and spectrographs. The cameras don't use photographic film, but rather electronic detectors like those used in video cameras. The spectrographs collect data by separating starlight into its rainbow of colors, as a prism does to sunlight. By closely studying these colors, astronomers can decode the star's temperature, motion, composition, and age.

The Hubble Space Telescope is as large as a school bus and looks like a five-story tower of stacked silver canisters. Each canister contains important telescopic equipment: the focusing mirrors, computers, imaging instruments, and pointing and control mechanisms. Solar panels for generating electricity, and antennas for communicating with operators on the ground, extend from the telescope.

DESIGN FEATURES OF SUPPORT SYSTEMS MODULE

equipment bay
digital interface unit
reaction wheel assembly
communication system
computer
low-gain antenna
umbilical interface
sun sensors
high-gain antenna
forward shell
battery and charge controller
access door
aft shroud

PRIMARY MIRROR

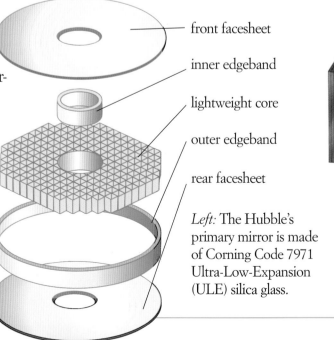

front facesheet
inner edgeband
lightweight core
outer edgeband
rear facesheet

Left: The Hubble's primary mirror is made of Corning Code 7971 Ultra-Low-Expansion (ULE) silica glass.

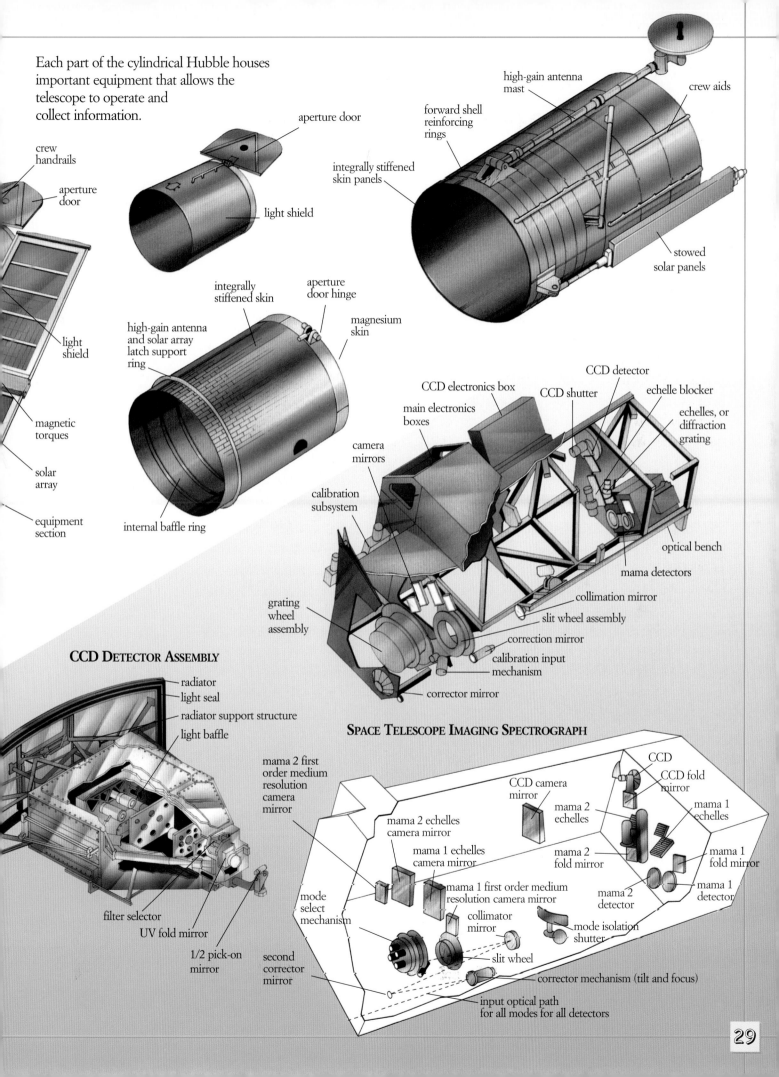

Each part of the cylindrical Hubble houses important equipment that allows the telescope to operate and collect information.

crew handrails

aperture door

light shield

magnetic torques

solar array

equipment section

aperture door

light shield

integrally stiffened skin

high-gain antenna and solar array latch support ring

internal baffle ring

aperture door hinge

magnesium skin

high-gain antenna mast

forward shell reinforcing rings

integrally stiffened skin panels

crew aids

stowed solar panels

CCD electronics box

main electronics boxes

camera mirrors

calibration subsystem

grating wheel assembly

CCD detector

CCD shutter

echelle blocker

echelles, or diffraction grating

optical bench

mama detectors

collimation mirror

slit wheel assembly

correction mirror

calibration input mechanism

corrector mirror

CCD DETECTOR ASSEMBLY

radiator

light seal

radiator support structure

light baffle

filter selector

UV fold mirror

1/2 pick-on mirror

second corrector mirror

SPACE TELESCOPE IMAGING SPECTROGRAPH

mama 2 first order medium resolution camera mirror

mama 2 echelles camera mirror

mama 1 echelles camera mirror

mode select mechanism

CCD camera mirror

mama 2 echelles

mama 1 first order medium resolution camera mirror

collimator mirror

slit wheel

CCD

CCD fold mirror

mama 2 fold mirror

mama 2 detector

mama 1 echelles

mama 1 fold mirror

mama 1 detector

mode isolation shutter

corrector mechanism (tilt and focus)

input optical path for all modes for all detectors

29

Stamps with HST images in honor of the great astronomer Edwin Powell Hubble. *Courtesy of NASA.*

The Hubble Space Telescope History

A RUGGED PATH TO THE STARS

Princeton University physicist Lyman Spitzer proposed the idea of a space telescope in the late 1940s as part of a U.S. government study of applications for space exploration. In response, NASA launched several small space telescopes in the late 1960s and early 1970s. They imagined putting a big, 118-inch (3-m) mirror in space called the Large Space Telescope (LST). Because of funding problems, the mirror was scaled back to 7.87 feet (2.4 m). The telescope was sold to Congress as valuable cargo for the newly built space shuttle, which determined the design for the telescope. It would need to fit into the shuttle cargo bay and be maintained by astronauts, as mechanics fix a car. Astronauts would have to visit the telescope every few years. This meant that the telescope needed to be placed in a low, Earth orbit at an altitude of 360 miles (579 km). However, this is not the ideal place for viewing the heavens, because Earth blocks the view of the sky for half of each orbit made by the Hubble.

Because of NASA budget problems, Congress almost canceled the space telescope twice, but lobbying campaigns by astronomers saved it. Then in the early 1980s, the telescope's construction had serious budget overruns. This caused engineers to cut corners on testing the telescope's complex design and optics. These short cuts would later come back to haunt NASA when an embarrassing flaw was discovered in the telescope's optics.

DIAGRAM SHOWING HOW SCIENTISTS COMMUNICATE WITH THE HUBBLE

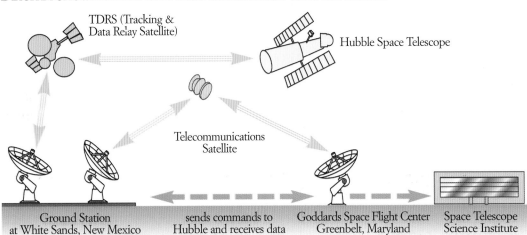

TDRS (Tracking & Data Relay Satellite)

Hubble Space Telescope

Telecommunications Satellite

Ground Station at White Sands, New Mexico — sends commands to Hubble and receives data — Goddards Space Flight Center Greenbelt, Maryland — Space Telescope Science Institute

Above: Orbiting Earth at an altitude of 356 nautical miles (659 km) perched atop a foot restraint on the space shuttle *Endeavor*'s remote manipulator system arm, astronauts F. Story Musgrave (top) and Jeffrey A. Hoffman complete the final of five extravehicular activities, or activities taking place outside the Hubble. The west coast of Australia forms the backdrop in this photograph.

FIXING HUBBLE

After the Hubble was launched in 1990, scientists discovered that its primary mirror was too shallow at the edge by 1/50 the width of a hair. This resulted in the blurring of starlight, because the telescope could not bring all the light to a single focus. Using image-processing techniques, scientists were able to subtract much of the blurriness, but only for moderately bright, nearby objects. Nevertheless, the Hubble's images, even when broken, still exceeded what could be seen with even bigger, ground-based telescopes. Therefore scientists were able to do significant research with the Hubble while an optical repair was being developed.

NASA and astronomers wrestled to find a solution for the embarrassing situation. NASA managers reported to Congress that the shuttle's servicing capabilities offered a sort of "insurance policy" for the Hubble. Replacement instruments could be outfitted with corrective lenses to make up for the primary mirror's blurry vision. It was like putting contact lenses on someone with poor vision.

Riccardo Giacconi, the Space Telescope Science Institute director, gathered a panel of astronomers to look at all the possibilities for fixing the Hubble. The best idea for the fix was inspired by a European hotel shower. Engineer Jim Crocker was fascinated by the design of the showerhead. Unlike American showers, this one could tilt and rotate up, down, and sideways, like the joystick on a computer game. He imagined little mirrors that could pivot and tilt to capture the light from the Hubble's misshapen primary mirror, correct it, and then send it to the instruments. He led the design of a device called the Corrective Optics Space Telescope Axial Replacement (COSTAR). The quarter-size mirrors on COSTAR would be misshapen in the opposite direction of the primary mirror flaw. This means they would reconstruct the light from the Hubble's primary mirror so that it was in crisp focus. In December 1993, the first Hubble servicing mission carried replacement instruments, including COSTAR, aboard the space shuttle *Endeavor* to fix the telescope.

The Hubble is about to be lifted into the vertical position in Kennedy Space Center's vertical processing facility.

Subaru and Gemini

THE SUBARU TELESCOPE IN HAWAII

Japan's Subaru Telescope is an optical-infrared telescope at Mauna Kea, Hawaii. The Subaru holds perhaps the unbeatable record of being the largest single-piece mirror ever made. Its 326-inch (8.3-m) mirror is only 10 inches (30 cm) thick. Two hundred sixty-one little plungers, or actuators, the most for any single mirror, help the thin mirror hold its shape. It took four years to complete the creation of the primary mirror, including drilling 261 holes for actuators on the back surface of the blank and polishing the front surface.

The telescope's building has a cylindrical shape, like a soda can, rather than the more common dome shape. The building was developed from computer simulations, or models, which estimated the stress of winds atop the mountain. The cylindrical shape prevents warm and turbulent outside air from entering. It also allows warm air produced inside the building to escape rapidly into the air outside the telescope.

SPANNING BOTH HEMISPHERES— THE TWIN GEMINI TELESCOPES

An identical pair of 315-inch (8-m) telescopes scan the northern and the southern skies for optical and infrared light. Gemini North is located atop Mauna Kea in Hawaii. Its twin, Gemini South, is at Cerro Pachón in northern Chile. Like other giant telescopes, each Gemini primary mirror rests on a bed of 120 actuators—circular supports the size of coffee cups that operate individually to move the primary mirror up and down no more than 1/410,000 the width of a human hair. Gemini also uses state-of-the-art adaptive optics. At the heart of the system is a 3-inch (7.6-cm) flexible mirror that changes shape 1,000 times per second to counteract the blurriness in starlight and make extremely sharp images. The twin telescopes work together to give a picture of the whole night sky.

Left: Inside of Subaru's primary focus camera with 6 CCOs installed

Below: The Subaru primary mirror is undergoing tests on the mirror cell. The 261 actuators supporting the primary mirror can be seen through the mirror.

Photos courtesy of Subaru Observatory.

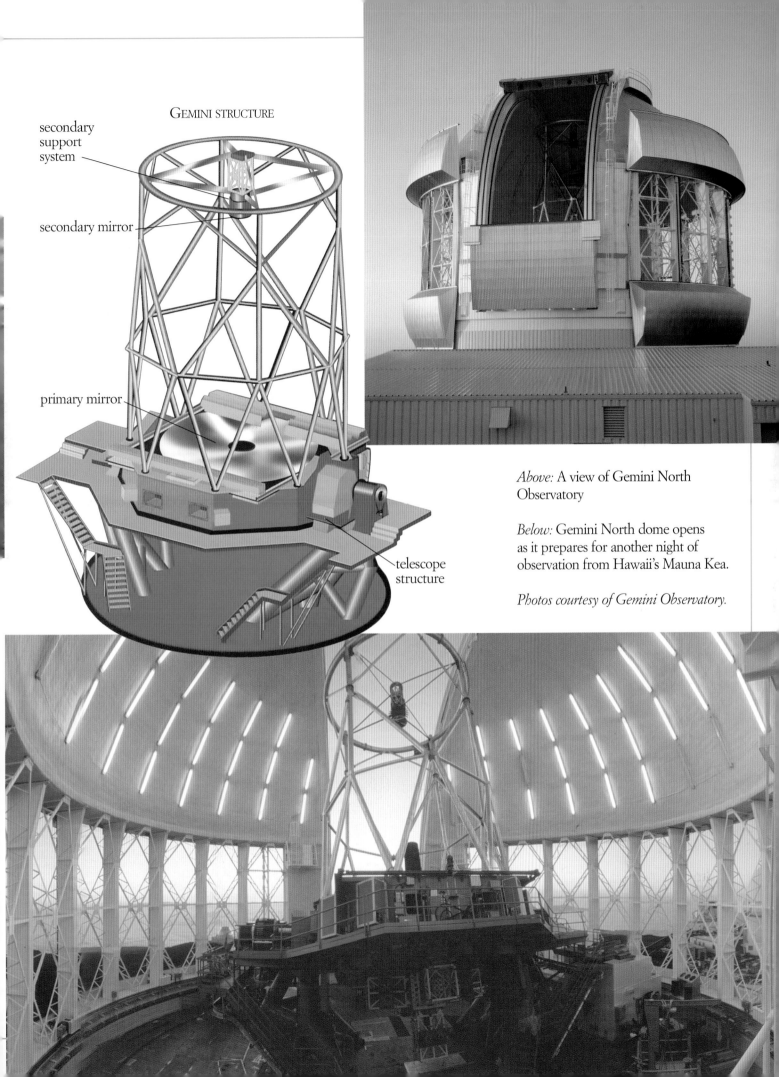

GEMINI STRUCTURE

secondary support system

secondary mirror

primary mirror

telescope structure

Above: A view of Gemini North Observatory

Below: Gemini North dome opens as it prepares for another night of observation from Hawaii's Mauna Kea.

Photos courtesy of Gemini Observatory.

Hobby-Eberly, Robotic Telescopes, and Keck I and II

HOBBY-EBERLY

Located in the rolling, dry Davis Mountains of western Texas, the Hobby-Eberly Telescope (HET) contains the world's largest multisegment primary mirror, measuring 433 inches (11 m) from edge to edge. Because of the way the Hobby-Eberly Telescope is used, only 362 inches (9.2 m) of its surface collect starlight at any given time. This makes the Hobby-Eberly Telescope the third-largest telescope in the world. To reduce the cost and the complexity of aiming such a huge telescope, it does not pivot up and down like a cannon. Instead it rotates a full 360 degrees on inflatable air-bearings on a huge concrete pier, probably the flattest piece of concrete of its size in the world.

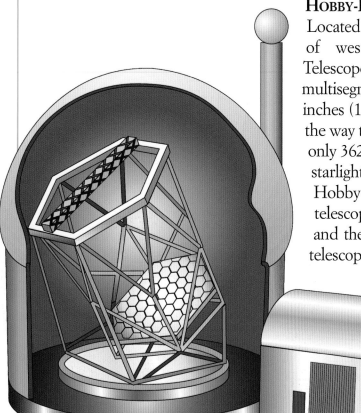

Left: This is a drawing of Hobby-Eberly Telescope structure.

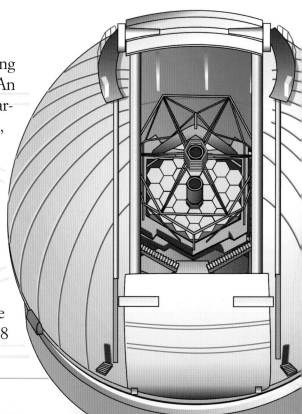

KECK II

ROBOTIC TELESCOPES

Catching sight of unexpected celestial fireworks, such as exploding stars, comets, or erupting black holes, is difficult for astronomers. An astronomer usually spends only a few nights per year looking at a particular selection of celestial targets. To avoid missing big events, astronomers have built robotic telescopes to act like surveillance cameras in a department store. Sitting alone and untended on mountaintops, they patrol the night sky, looking for any changes from the far corners of the universe. They move quickly and precisely, relying on their own onboard computers and sky maps to prowl the heavens. The nightly flood of data is automatically analyzed to look for any changes in the universe. The largest robotic telescope so far is the 78-inch (2 m) Liverpool Robotic Telescope, located in La Palma in Spain's Canary Islands, located off the Northwest coast of Africa. The control center is 2,000 miles (3,218 km) away in Great Britain.

HAWAII'S KECK TELESCOPES

Resembling a pair of monstrous, mutant fly's eyes, the Keck I and Keck II telescopes are the kings of the mountain in Mauna Kea, Hawaii. The eighty-seven-million-dollar Keck I and the seventy-seven-million-dollar Keck II telescopes were built as a joint venture among the California Institute of Technology, the University of California, and the W.M. Keck Foundation of Los Angeles, California. Each telescope stands eight stories tall and weighs 300 tons (272 t). Giant air conditioners run constantly during the day, keeping the dome temperature at or below freezing. At night when the dome is opened, exposing each telescope to the frigid night air, the telescopes are already at outdoor temperature. During observation, a computer-controlled system of sensors and actuators adjusts the position of each of the thirty-six mirror segments on each telescope to an accuracy of 1/1,000th the thickness of a human hair! This twice-per-second adjustment counters the tug of gravity on the immense mirror assembly. Light collected by the twin Keck telescopes will eventually be combined to provide the equivalent sharpness of a 278-foot (85-m) telescope. To improve the telescopes' sharpness further, four smaller 6-foot (1.8-m) telescopes will be placed around the two Keck telescopes. A sophisticated optical system will precisely combine the light received simultaneously by the six telescopes.

Below: Light entering the telescope is concentrated by the curved primary mirror, reflected to the secondary and tertiary (or third) mirrors, and then reflected into the optical instruments. In infrared observing, a special secondary mirror reflects the light directly back to the infrared instruments, replacing the optical tertiary mirror.

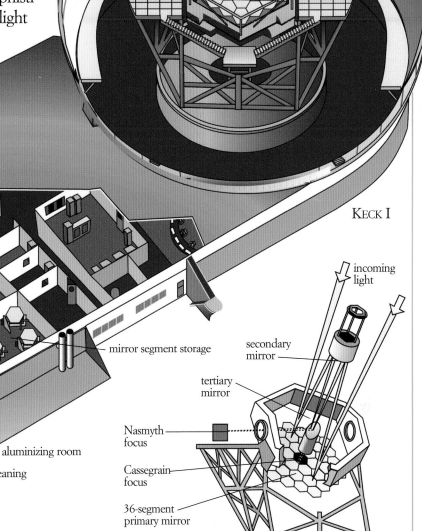

KECK I

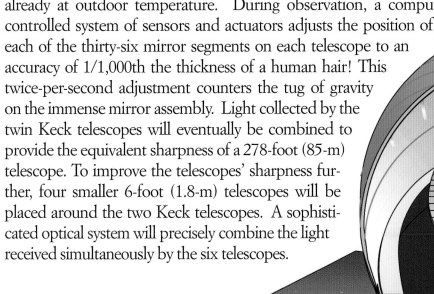

mirror segment storage

aluminizing room

mirror segment cleaning

Keck II computer

Keck II control room

incoming light

secondary mirror

tertiary mirror

Nasmyth focus

Cassegrain focus

36-segment primary mirror

The Very Large Telescope and the Binocular

Among the most interesting characteristics of VLT is the possibility of its being used as an interferometer. With its four large telescopes and two or three smaller, auxiliary telescopes, VLT will have the viewing power and image resolution equal to that of a single telescope 656 feet (200 m) in diameter.

Below: The VLT is under construction in the huge Ansaldo hangar in Milan, Italy.
Courtesy of ESO.

Left: The top of Cerro Panal with four VLT telescopes.

VERY LARGE TELESCOPE

Resembling a modern-day version of an ancient Aztec city, the world's most powerful optical observatory is the Very Large Telescope (VLT). Four gigantic observatory buildings sit in a magnificent row, like silent sentinels, at the summit of 8,635-foot (2,632-m) Cerro Paranal, about 90 miles (144.8 km) south of Antofagasta, Chile. Engineers originally thought about using inflatable domes to protect each of the giant telescopes from the wind, but they decided on cylindrical buildings.

Each of the four telescopes has a gigantic, 314-inch (8-m) mirror. The Schott Glaswerke Company in Mainz, Germany, spun cast the mirrors from an Ultra-Low-Expansion glass that allows the mirror to hold its shape as the temperature changes. REOSC Optics in France polished the mirrors. Each mirror is no more than about 8 inches (20 cm) thick and weighs about 50,000 pounds (18 t). The mirrors are supported in a cradle that continually adjusts for any flexing of the mirror. The telescopes are named Antu, Kueyen, Melipal, and Yepun, the names of the Sun, the Moon, the Southern Cross, and the star Sirius, in the local Mapudungo Indian language. When needed, the light from four gigantic mirrors will be combined to give the VLT extra light-gathering power and sharpness. If your eyes could see as sharply as these telescopes, you could see headlights on a car that was 400,000 miles (644,000 km) away—more than 1.5 times the distance of Earth from the Moon!

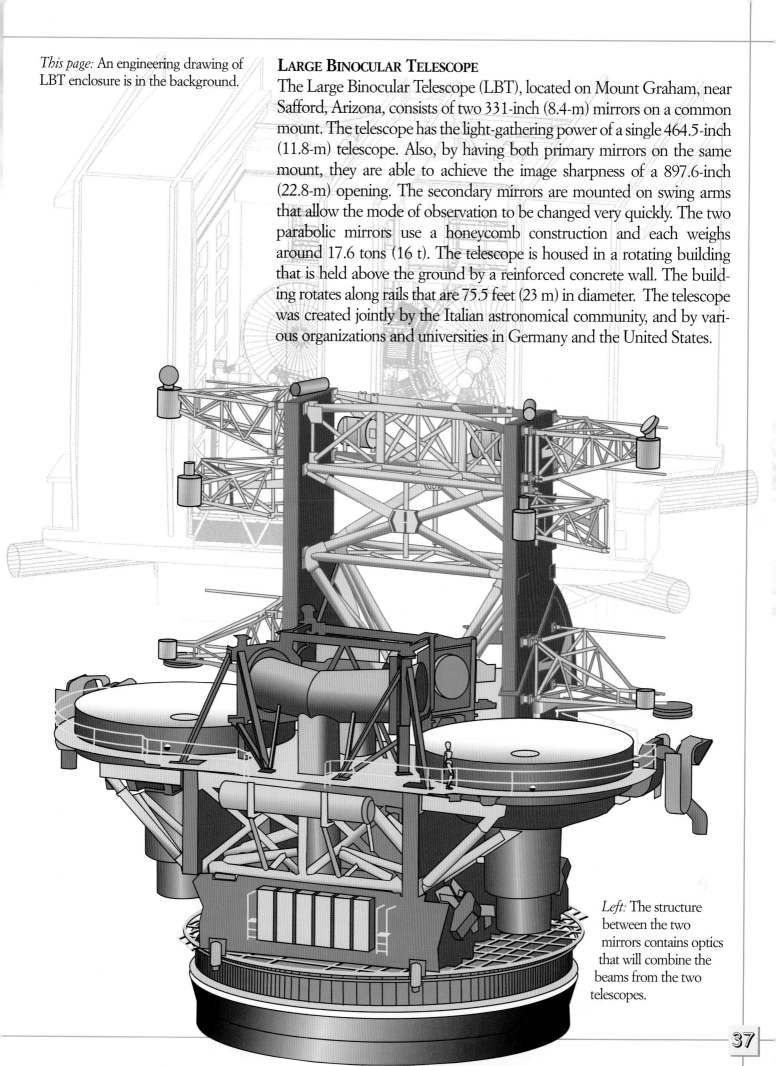

This page: An engineering drawing of LBT enclosure is in the background.

LARGE BINOCULAR TELESCOPE

The Large Binocular Telescope (LBT), located on Mount Graham, near Safford, Arizona, consists of two 331-inch (8.4-m) mirrors on a common mount. The telescope has the light-gathering power of a single 464.5-inch (11.8-m) telescope. Also, by having both primary mirrors on the same mount, they are able to achieve the image sharpness of a 897.6-inch (22.8-m) opening. The secondary mirrors are mounted on swing arms that allow the mode of observation to be changed very quickly. The two parabolic mirrors use a honeycomb construction and each weighs around 17.6 tons (16 t). The telescope is housed in a rotating building that is held above the ground by a reinforced concrete wall. The building rotates along rails that are 75.5 feet (23 m) in diameter. The telescope was created jointly by the Italian astronomical community, and by various organizations and universities in Germany and the United States.

Left: The structure between the two mirrors contains optics that will combine the beams from the two telescopes.

The Invisible Universe

RADIO TELESCOPES

Popular culture and Hollywood movies like *Contact* make people think of sounds when they see a picture of a radio telescope. Radio astronomers do not actually listen to noises. Sound and radio waves are two different phenomena. Sound consists of variations in air or water pressure and does not travel through the vacuum of space. Radio waves, like visible light, travel through space at the speed of light: 186,000 miles per second (300,000 km/s). When you turn on a radio, you hear sounds because the transmitter at the radio station encodes radio waves to make them carry information about voices and music. Your radio tuner receives the radio waves, decodes this information, and changes it back into audible sounds. Radio telescopes are designed to produce images of celestial bodies. Just as photographic film records the different amount of light coming from different parts of the scene viewed by a camera's lens, radio telescopes record the different amounts of radio energy coming from the universe. After a computer processes this information, astronomers can make a picture.

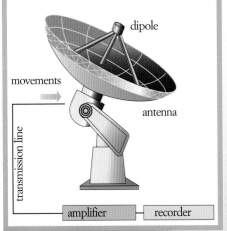

One of the largest radio telescopes is the Very Large Array (VLA) near Socorro, New Mexico. It is a Y-shaped array of twenty-seven dish antennas, each 81 feet (25 m) across. The antennas extend over a region of 22 miles (35 km) across. By combining the signals from all the telescopes, the VLA can see objects 1,000 times sharper than optical telescopes.

In 1895, the German physicist Wilhelm Roentgen discovered a mysterious new form of energy that he called X rays. He realized this powerful radiation had the ability to pass through many materials that block visible light. X rays eventually were found to be just another form of light, though far more energetic and penetrating.

In the 1960s, simple X-ray detectors were mounted on high-altitude rockets. Astronomers were surprised to see X rays streaming from flares on stars, white dwarfs, neutron stars, black holes, and many other objects.

Because of their high energy, X rays will ricochet off mirrors. Therefore, X-ray telescopes must be very different from optical telescopes. They look more like glass barrels than the familiar dish shape of optical telescopes. NASA's Chandra X ray Observatory is now the most powerful X-ray telescope ever built. It has made a number of exciting discoveries including the amazing fact that, long ago, the universe was full of monstrous black holes.

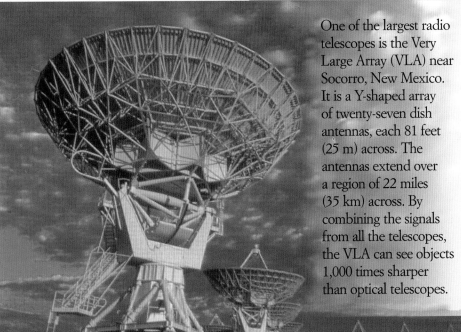

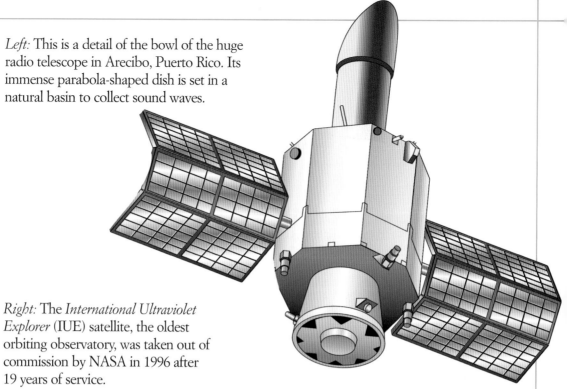

Left: This is a detail of the bowl of the huge radio telescope in Arecibo, Puerto Rico. Its immense parabola-shaped dish is set in a natural basin to collect sound waves.

Right: The *International Ultraviolet Explorer* (IUE) satellite, the oldest orbiting observatory, was taken out of commission by NASA in 1996 after 19 years of service.

The basic design of a radio telescope is similar to that of an optical telescope. A big, bowl-shaped dish collects radiation from space and brings it to a focus to make an image. The energy these telescopes pick up and record from distant sources is very weak, less than the energy released when a snowflake hits the ground! Radio telescopes must be much bigger than optical ones because they are looking at longer wavelengths of electromagnetic radiation. Radio waves are typically between 3 feet (1 m) and .5 mile (.8 km) in length. Light waves are only about one 1/10,000 of an inch (cm) long. This means that radio telescopes do not need to have as smooth a surface as optical telescopes do, so they often are made of simple steel and wire mesh.

Another difference between optical telescopes and radio telescopes is that radio telescope observations can take place all day long. It doesn't have to be dark outside. Also, instead of being on mountaintops, these telescopes must be located in valleys and other areas naturally shielded from human-made radio waves. The Big Ear, the largest radio telescope dish, built into a bowl-shaped valley in Arecibo, Puerto Rico, is 1,000 feet (305 m) across.

The VLA is dwarfed by the Very Long Baseline Interferometer (VLBI), consisting of ten dish-shaped antennas, each 82 feet (25 m) in diameter, spread out between Hawaii and the U.S. Virgin Islands. The VLBI is equivalent to a single telescope almost 5,000 miles (8,046 km) across! Planned for the remote Atacama Desert in Chile is an "orchard" of sixty-four radio antennas, each 39 feet (12 m) wide. They will work together like one gigantic eye as wide as 10 miles (16 km) across. Called the Atacama Large Millimeter Array (ALMA), these telescopes will study the birth of galaxies, the structure of our universe, and the birth of planets.

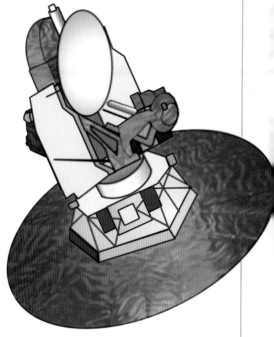

Above: The Microwave Anistropy Probe (MAP) is a NASA *Explorer* mission that will measure the anistropy, or changes in temperature, of the cosmic background radiation over the full sky with greater accuracy than possible ever before. This map of the left-over heat from the big bang will give us answers to fundamental questions about the origin of our universe.

Observatories Around the World

HOME FOR A TELESCOPE

Finding a site to build and to operate a telescope is one of the biggest challenges in astronomy. For many celestial observations, weather must be clear most of the year. The air above the telescope must be free from turbulence. If the air is turbulent, an astronomer may have to wait as long as a year for the opportunity to observe the same celestial target. Even when the sky is clear, the humidity needs to be low, otherwise the sky will have a slight haze that reduces image sharpness. Water vapor also interferes with observations. Therefore, telescope sites need to be in arid parts of the world. The site also must be far away from the light pollution of major cities. Intense darkness can be enjoyed in only

HAWAIIAN ISLANDS

Headquarters
Kamuela

Observatories
Mauna Kea

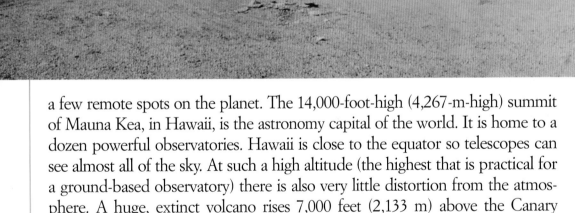

a few remote spots on the planet. The 14,000-foot-high (4,267-m-high) summit of Mauna Kea, in Hawaii, is the astronomy capital of the world. It is home to a dozen powerful observatories. Hawaii is close to the equator so telescopes can see almost all of the sky. At such a high altitude (the highest that is practical for a ground-based observatory) there is also very little distortion from the atmosphere. A huge, extinct volcano rises 7,000 feet (2,133 m) above the Canary Islands. It is another one of the finest sites in the world, with four telescopes, including the 165-inch (4.2-m) William Herschel Telescope.

Australia's top site for viewing the southern sky is located at an altitude of nearly 4,000 feet (1,220 m) on Siding Spring Mountain in New South Wales. The observatory has a 153-inch (3.9-m) reflecting telescope, one of the largest in the world. The Atacama Desert in northern Chile is one of the most barren places on Earth but is home to one of the leading observatories, the Very Large Telescope. The Sonoran Desert in Arizona is home to the National Optical Astronomy Observatory's Kitt Peak National Observatory. A total of twenty-two optical and two radio telescopes are on the 6,875-foot (2,095-m) mountaintop.

Above: This is the site of Llano de Chajnantor near the village of San Pedro in the Atacama Desert in Chile. At an altitude of 16,404 feet (5,000 m), it is the highest point ever chosen for an astrophysical observatory. The clear sky and dry air are favorable for radio astronomy as well as for optical telescope observations.
Courtesy of ESO.

1 MAUNA KEA OBSERVATORIES, Hawaii, USA
2 LAS CAMPANAS OBSERVATORY, Ceroo Las Campanas, Chile
3 OBSERVATORIO DEL ROQUE DE LOS MUCHACHOS,
   Isla de La Palma, Canary Islands, Spain
4 ESO'S PARANAL OBSERVATORY, Cerro Paranal, Chile
5 ESO LA SILLA OBSERVATORY, La Silla, Chile
6 OSSERVATORIO INTER-AMERICANO, Cerro Totolo, Chile
7 SIDING SPRING OBSERVATORY, New South Wales, Australia
8 McDONALD OBSERVATORY, Texas, USA
9 FRED LAWRENCE WHIPPLE OBSERVATORY, Arizona, USA
10 KITT PEAK NATIONAL OBSERVATORY, Arizona, USA
11 MT. GRAHAM INTERNATIONAL OBSERVATORY, Arizona, USA
12 PALOMAR OBSERVATORY, California, USA
13 OSSERVATORIO DI CALAR ALTO, Spain
14 LICK OBSERVATORY, California, USA
15 BYURAKAN ASTROPHYSICAL OBSERVATORY, Armenia
16 YERKES OBSERVATORY, Wisconsin, USA
17 SPECIAL ASTROPHYSICAL OBSERVATORY, Russia
18 CRIMEAN ASTROPHYSICAL OBSERVATORY, Ukraine
19 KARL-SCHWARZSCHILD OBSERVATORIUM, Tautenberg, Germany
20 OBSERVATORIO ASTRONOMICALNACIONAL, Alcalá de
   Henares, Spain

These maps and the key show where some of the
major observatories around the world are located.
In every case, the telescopes are located in remote
places. Isolated sites mean that telescope parts must
be carried over poor roads, and astronomers have
a long way to travel to visit the telescopes
and make observations.

3.6-m Telescope
and 1.4-m C.T.A.
tower

1.5-m Swedish
E.S.O. Telescope

3.58-m NTT
Telescope

Astronomical
Laboratory

1.52-m Schmidt
Telescope

2.2-m Telescope

1.54-m Danish

40-cm G.P.O.
Telescope

1.04-m Photometric Telescope

91-cm Dutch
Telescope

1.52-m Spectrographic
Telescope

50-cm Bochum
Telescope

50-cm Danish
Telescope

LA SILLA, CHILE

This map
shows the many
observatories
located in
La Silla, Chile.

The Future

MEGATELESCOPES

One of the possible directions the future of telescopes might take is the creation of megatelescopes. To create these huge telescopes, technology from existing telescopes will need to be taken to the next level. For example, the success of the Keck Telescope multimirror design has opened the door for ever-larger, ground-based telescopes with mirrors half the size of a U.S. football field! These megatelescopes will use the same basic segmented mirror design that has proven so successful in the Keck. They are expected to cost between five hundred million and one billion dollars to build. To be affordable and workable, megatelescopes will also require technological advances so that lightweight mirror segments can be mass-produced, like cars off an assembly line. The structures housing the mirrors will be as big across as the Eiffel Tower and almost half as tall!

The proposed California Extremely Large Telescope (CELT) will have a whopping 1,080 hexagonal mirror segments! Even bigger is the Overwhelmingly Large Telescope (OWL), under study by the European Southern Observatory, which will require 2,058 segments. To be built in a reasonable amount of time, the 328-foot (100-m) diameter OWL must use simpler mass-produced mirror tiles, but will have to make do with a less-than-perfect shape and poorer optical quality. This will have to be corrected by additional mirrors that catch the light coming from the large primary mirror. All megatelescopes will need adaptive optics to keep the images sharp.

NEXT GENERATION SPACE TELESCOPE

Planned to be launched in 2009, NASA's Next Generation Space Telescope (NGST) will look to the farthest reaches of space to see the very first stars and galaxies that were ever born. To do this, it must be able to collect infrared light that has been traveling across space since nearly the beginning of time. This means putting a telescope in space that has a mirror at least 255 inches (6.5 m) across. NGST will enjoy the Hubble's crystal-clear view of an ultra-black sky, but will have much sharper vision. In the cold vacuum of space, it will be easy to keep NGST cooled to a frigid -280°F (-137°C), the temperature needed for picking up faint infrared light. Unlike the Hubble, NGST will not be upgradeable or repairable because astronauts will not be able to visit it. The telescope will be located in a special parking orbit 1 million miles (1.6 million km) beyond Earth.

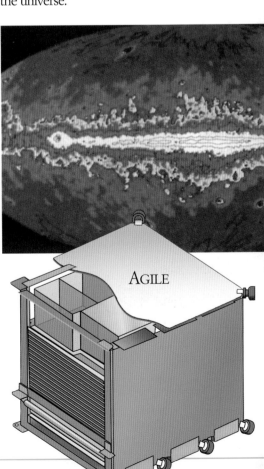

Above: The Gamma Ray Large Area Space Telescope (GLAST) is a next generation high-energy gamma-ray observatory. Gamma rays are more than a billion times more energetic than radiation, or light visible to human eyes. GLAST, planned to launch in 2005, is designed to look, with much greater detail and accuracy, at the many mysteries in space that are visible through gamma-rays, such as what is happening in supermassive black holes or the cause of high-energy gamma-ray bursts. This telescope will also help scientists gain more information about the formation of the universe.

AGILE

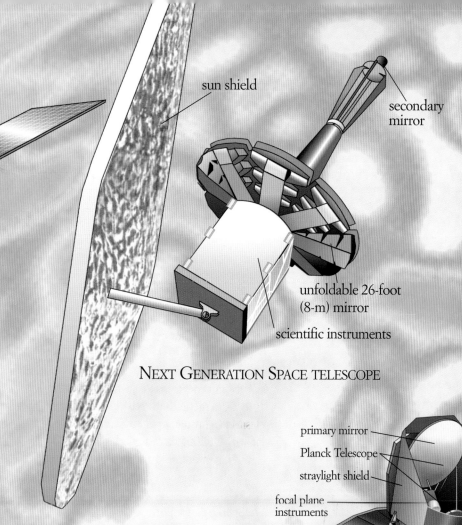

sun shield

secondary mirror

unfoldable 26-foot (8-m) mirror

scientific instruments

NEXT GENERATION SPACE TELESCOPE

Background: An image of our galaxy obtained by the Differential Microwave Radiometer (DMR) developer used by COBE Satellite Observatory.

NEXT GENERATION SPACE TELESCOPE (NGST)

The Next Generation Space Telescope (NGST) will be the successor to the Hubble Space Telescope and may be launched as early as 2007. NGST will be used for discovering and understanding the formation of the first stars and galaxies, the evolution of galaxies, and the star and planet formation. The NGST will be located 1 million miles beyond the Moon.

primary mirror

Planck Telescope

straylight shield

focal plane instruments

thermal shields

interface to FIRST

service module shields

service module

solar array

THE PLANCK SATELLITE

LOOKING BACK TO THE DAWN OF TIME The *Planck* satellite, a mission of the European Space Agency due to be launched in 2007, is one of the most ambitious projects yet for answering questions about the origin of the universe. *Planck* is currently being designed by astronomers all around Europe to help to solve many of the big questions still pending in cosmology. This satellite will study the Cosmic Microwave Background radiation by measuring its temperature all over the sky. *Planck*'s large telescope will collect the light from the Cosmic Microwave Background and will focus it onto two arrays of radio detectors, which will translate the signal into a temperature.

Left, bottom: The Italian telescope *Astrorivelatore Gamma a Immagini Leggero* (AGILE) will be operational in 2003. It will be able to observe surges of energy 1,000 times weaker than gamma rays and to establish in a very precise way the position of celestial objects in space. In addition, it will have a clear view of a fifth of the sky and will allow the astrophysical community around the world to observe and study some of the most violent phenomenon in the cosmos.

ALMA PROJECT

Left: This is a schematic drawing of the Atacama Large Millimeter Array (ALMA) project to be located in Chile. The largest astronomical project in the world, it will unite European, American, and Japanese interests. ALMA will be constructed between 2002 and 2008 and will consist of 64 antennas. Millimeter astronomy gives great detail about the history of the universe, as light and radiation given off in celestial activity fades into millimeter and submillimeter radiation. ALMA will be able to view this radiation and will give a new and detailed picture of the universe.

Glossary

active optics (AK-tiv OP-tiks) A system that automatically modifies one or more mirrors in a telescope to correct for atmospheric turbulence.

adaptive optics (uh-DAP-tiv OP-tiks) A system that automatically and continuously adjusts the physical shape of a telescope mirror to keep it in focus.

aft shroud (AFT SHROWD) The covering at the back of a ship.

aluminize (uh-LOO-mih-nyz) To coat something in aluminum, a metal that is a good conductor of electricity and heat and that reflects light well.

aperture (AP-er-chur) The opening in a lens that admits the light, especially in a camera.

auxiliary (og-ZIL-yuh-ree) Supplementary, or serving in a supporting fashion, rather than in a main one.

axial (AK-see-ul) Something that runs in the same direction as the axis, or perpendicular to the plane of a circular object.

baffle (BA-ful) A device, like a plate, a screen, or a wall, that is used to deflect or to control the flow of something, such as light.

bay (BAY) A compartment or section of a structure such as a satellite or a spacecraft.

big bang (BIG BANG) The theory that the universe was born from an extremely hot and dense fireball.

black hole (BLAK HOHL) An incredibly massive and dense object in space where gravity is so strong that nothing—not even light—can escape.

Cassegrain focus (CA-seg-rayn FO-kus) In a telescope, the manner in which the light is reflected using a secondary mirror to sharpen and to redirect the light to the eyepiece.

Charge-Coupled Device (CCD) (CHARJ KUh-puld dih-VYS) A solid-state silicon chip, typically the size of a matchbook or postage stamp, which converts light to an electronic signal. The signal is used to reconstruct an image of the light collected.

The CCD is divided into many picture elements. The more elements there are, the sharper the image.

collimator (KAH-lih-may-ter) A device that produces beams of parallel rays of light.

corrective foil (kuh-REK-tiv FOYL) A thin piece of metal, or another material, used to correct light as it enters a telescope.

coudé focus (koo-DAY FOH-kus) A telescope that is constructed so that the light is reflected along a polar axis to come to a focus at the place where a photographic plate or a spectrograph is mounted.

diffraction (dih-FRAK-shun) The dividing of light into its component colors.

diffraction grating (dih-FRAK-shun GRAYT-ing) A mirror that has been finely etched with many microscopic parallel lines. The lines break up starlight to make a spectrum or rainbow of colors.

echelles (eh-SHELLZ) Diffraction grating.

electromagnetic radiation (ih-lek-troh-mag-NEH-tik ray-dee-AY-shun) Waves of energy from gamma-ray to radio energy that travel across space. They are created inside atoms.

equatorial axis (ee-kwa-TOR-ee-ul AK-sis) A support that is in the same direction as Earth's axis.

eyepiece (EYE-pees) A small magnifying lens used for enlarging the image at the focus of a telescope.

field of view (FEELD UV VYOO) A measure of how much sky a telescope sees. Many telescopes have a field of view smaller than the diameter of the full moon as seen in the sky.

filaments (FIH-luh-ments) Thin, threadlike pieces of metal that give off light when electricity passes through them.

focal length (FOH-kul LENKTH) The distance a beam of light travels through a telescope before it comes to a focus.

focus (FOH-kus) The location where all the light rays gathered in a telescope come together.

folded optics (FOHLD-ed OP-tiks) The mechanisms in a telescope, such as primary and secondary mirrors that reflect light in such a way that its path folds back and increases the focal length of the telescope.

galaxy (GA-luk-see) A large system of about one hundred billion stars. Our sun is a member of the Milky Way galaxy. There are billions of galaxies in the observable universe.

gamma ray (GA-muh RAY) A high-energy photon, or light particle, released by something radioactive.

gigabyte (JIH-guh-byt) A billion bytes of computer data, or one thousand megabytes.

hyperbola (hi-PUR-buh-luh) A complex curve used in telescope mirrors requiring a shorter focal length.

infrared (in-fruh-RED) Radiation outside the visible spectrum of colors at the red end. Photographic film and CCDs are sensitive to infrared radiation that is invisible to the human eye.

interferometer (in-ter-fuh-RAH-muh-ter) A device that uses information about how waves, such as light waves, interfere with each other to make precise determinations about an observed object.

light (LYT) That portion of the electromagnetic radiation to which our eyes are sensitive.

light pollution (LYT puh-LOO-shun) The glare of light from cities that interferes with telescopic observations.

magnetic torque (mag-NEH-tik TORK) A device that provides power through rotation or twisting. The rotation is powered by attractive, or magentic, forces. This can power such things as wheels or engines.

meniscus mirrors (muh-NIS-kus MIR-urz) Meaning "membrane"; the term for an extremely thin mirror only inches thick but many feet across.

Nasmyth focus (NA-smith FO-kus) A type of focus for a telescope named for scientist and inventor James Nasmyth.

neutron star (NOO-tron STAR) The ultracompact core of a star that has exploded.

North Star (NORTH STAR) The star that is located directly above the North Pole. The star appears to stand still as Earth rotates. The star's proper name is Polaris.

optical telescope assembly (OP-tih-kul TEH-luh-skohp uh-SEM-blee) Term for the complete structure that houses all the optical components of a telescope.

orbit (OR-bit) The circular path a body follows around an object that has captured it gravitationally.

parabola (puh-RA-buh-luh) A mathematically simple, precise curve used as the basis of most primary mirror shapes.

phenomena (fih-NAH-muh-nuh) A fact or an event of scientific interest.

primary mirror (PRY-mer-ee MIR-ur) The largest mirror in a telescope for collecting starlight.

polar axis (POH-lur AK-sis) An axis or pivoting point or line parallel to Earth's North and South Poles.

quasar (KWAY-zar) A very distant, bright object believed to be a giant black hole in the center of a galaxy.

reflector (rih-FLEK-ter) A telescope that uses a concave mirror for collecting light.

refraction (rih-FRAK-shun) The bending of starlight by glass or some other transparent medium.

refractor (rih-FRAK-ter) A telescope that uses a lens for collecting light.

resolve (rih-ZOLV) The act of distinguishing between two nearby objects.

satellite (SA-ti-lyt) An object, natural or human-made, that orbits a planet.

seeing (SEE-ing) An astronomer's term for describing how clear and steady the atmosphere is for making observations.

segmented mirror (SEG-ment-id MIR-ur) A large telescope mirror assembled from many smaller pieces that are individually ground and polished.

shutter (SHUH-ter) A mechanical device, especially

Glossary

on a camera or a telescope, that limits the passage of light.

solder (SAW-der) The process of uniting different things, usually by melting metal to join other metallic pieces.

space race (SPAYS RAYS) The technological competition between the United States and former Soviet Union to demonstrate political and military dominance over the use of space.

spectroscope (SPEK-truh-skohp) An instrument that splits apart light into its colors.

spectroscopy (spek-TROS-kuh-pee) The science of analyzing light that has been divided into its component's colors.

spin-cast (SPIN-KAST) Term for casting a mirror into a parabolic shape by rotating it as the glass cools.

Sputnik (SPUT-nik) The name of the first artificial satellite ever to be placed into an orbit around Earth.

telescope (TEH-luh-skohp) An instrument used to collect large amounts of light from faraway objects and to increase their visibility to the naked eye.

turbulent (TER-byuh-lent) Causing unrest, or irregular atmospheric movement.

ulraviolet (ul-truh-VY-let) Beyond the visible spectrum at the violet end; a wavelength between visible light and X rays.

vacuum chamber (VA-kyum CHAYM-bur) A container where most of the air is pumped out for research or technological applications, such as aluminizing a telescope mirror.

variable star (VAIR-ee-uh-bul STAR) A star that continually brightens and fades; typically an old star.

white dwarf (WHYT DWORF) A star like our sun that has burned out and shrunken.

Additional Resources

For additional information about large telescopes, check out the following books and Web sites:

Books

Schultz, Ron, and Nick Gadbois. *Looking Inside Telescopes and the Night Sky (X-Ray Vision)*. California: Avalon Travel Publsihing, 1992.

Simon, Seymour. *Out of Sight: Pictures of Hidden Worlds*. New York: Seastar Books, 2000.

Web Sites

www.astro.caltech.edu/mirror/keck/index.html
www.eso.org/
http://hubble.stsci.edu/
www.nasa.gov/
www.noao.edu/
www.nrao.edu/

Index

About the Author

Ray Villard has specialized in communicating astronomy to the public for the past twenty-eight years. He has received several NASA service awards for his contribution to the Hubble Telescope project. As Public Information Manager for the Space Telescope Science Institute at the Johns Hopkins University in Baltimore, Maryland, he is responsible for disseminating news about the most recent discoveries made with Hubble Space Telescope. He previously was associate editor for *Astronomy Magazine*, and *Star & Sky* magazine. He has written a variety of freelance articles for magazines, encyclopedias, and scripts for several syndicated science programs on public radio. Mr. Villard has scripted shows for several major planetariums and developed planetarium school programs. He teaches astronomy courses and hosts public seminars through the Johns Hopkins University, the Smithsonian Institution and Howard Community College in Columbia, MD. He holds an Master's of Science. degree in Science Communication from Boston University.

Photo Credits